Fair Ladies at a Game of Poem Cards

Two pairs of lovers are threatened with death by the jealousy of a cunning and powerful lord. But love is not easily crushed, and its ultimate triumph transforms the whole of society.

Peter Oswald's first stage piece, *The Swansong of Ivanhoe Westeway*, written while at university, was produced at the Edinburgh Festival and at the Brain Club, London, followed by two original verse plays, *Allbright* (1991) and *Valdorama* (1992). Other work includes versions of Schiller's *Don Carlos*, Sophocles' *Oedipus Tyrannos*, Plautus' *The Haunted House*, Tirso de Molina's *Don Juan*. His play, *Cinderella and the Coat of Skins*, premiered at the Battersea Arts Centre in 1996.

T0262483

Fair Ladies at a Game of Poem Cards

A verse play by
Peter Oswald

Based on an original by the
Kabuki 18th-century playwright
Chikamatsu Monzaemon

Methuen Drama

First published in Great Britain in 1996
by Methuen Drama

Copyright © 1996 by Peter Oswald
The author has asserted his moral rights

ISBN 0 413 71510 8

A CIP catalogue record for this book
is available from the British Library

Typeset by Wilmaset Ltd, Birkenhead, Wirral

Caution
All rights in this version are strictly reserved and applications
for performance etc. should be made to The Peters Fraser &
Dunlop Group Ltd, 503/4 The Chambers, Chelsea Harbour,
London SW10 0XF. No performance may be given unless a
licence has been obtained.

This paperback is sold subject to the condition that it shall not,
by way of trade or otherwise, be lent, resold, hired out, or
otherwise circulated without the publisher's prior consent in
any form of binding or cover other than that in which it is
published and without a similar condition being imposed on the
subsequent purchaser.

Fair Ladies at a Game of Poem Cards

Note

The director Tim Carroll, who in 1992 commissioned me to write a version of Schiller's *Don Carlos*, in 1994 presented me with *Fair Ladies at a Game of Poem Cards*, by Chikamatsu Monzaemon. He found it in an anthology in a second-hand bookshop in Dallas. Strangely, it wasn't set out like a play, but like an account of a play: mainly narration, some reported speech. This is because the original piece was written for puppets. Strange though it may seem, this eighteenth-century Japanese puppet play seemed to us the perfect vehicle for creating a twentieth-century English play in unrhyming pentameters.

I had written plays of my own in verse, with plots invented by me, and done a fair number of adaptations into verse – but this was the first time I had been presented with a storyline of proven strength on which to build. Perhaps this is the best way for verse playwriting to proceed. Certainly verse playwrights in the past have tended to use other people's stories more than prose playwrights have. In my case it felt like a breakthrough – here was romance, intrigue, courts, heroic journeys – all the things we know verse drama can work with. Yet the shadow of the Jacobeans had not touched the story – it was from a completely different culture. So one of my problems, that of writing in a Jacobean form without deferring too much to the Jacobeans, was overcome from the start. This left me free to write, I hope, in a contemporary style, though using a form that has fallen largely silent.

I didn't set out to write a play that was true to its Japanese origins. My only aim was to write a new play that worked in my chosen meter. I felt free to invent my own characters, and did so – the Titmouse, the Moon. Because Japanese dramatic style is more episodic than ours, the plot needed some reshaping to bring it into line with western expectations. The verse collected around a series of images of circles and widening spheres. In the intense dramatic situations Chikamatsu created, I felt no need to downplay the verse. On the contrary I felt that the imagery should be transcendent and full of blazing light. It seemed to me that the whole thing could be made into a kind of search for heaven.

I would like to thank Tim Carroll for providing me with the storyline for this work, for arranging a reading at the Northcott Theatre, Exeter, and for his support and dramaturgical assistance. I would also like to thank the National Studio for the reading they organised. And Chikamatsu.

Peter Oswald, November 1996

Fair Ladies at a Game of Poem Cards was first performed in the
Cottesloe auditorium of the Royal National Theatre,
London, on 14 November 1996. The cast was as follows:

Moon	Olwen Fouere
Titmouse	Luke Brown/Scott Charles
Lady Tonase	Naomi Wirthner
Lord Shigemori	Colin McFarlane
Takiguchi	Bohdan Poraj
Kojiju	Parminder K Nagra
Kohagi	Rebecca Thorn
Karumo	Rachel Power
Yokobue	Mairead McKinley
Lord Morotaka	David Haig
Empress Kenrei Mon-In	Olwen Fouere
Yoshitsugu	Adrian Irvine
Lord Katsuyori	Clive Merrison
Genjo	Clive Merrison
Lord Moritsugu	Sean Chapman
Peasant Girl	Rebecca Thorn
Servant	Sean Chapman
Kamawake	Luke Brown/Scott Charles
Muzo	Parminder K Nagra
Genkuro	Rebecca Thorn

Directed by John Crowley
Designed by Vicki Mortimer
Lighting by Rick Fisher
Music by Paddy Cunneen
Movement by Jonathan Butterell
Sound by Sue Patrick
Fights by Terry King

Characters

Takiguchi, *a young samurai*
Yokobue, *his lover, a maid of honour of the empress*
Yoshitsugu, *a young samurai*
Karumo, *his lover, colleague of Yokobue*
Lord Shigemori, *Lord High Keeper of the Privy Seal*
Empress Kenrei Mon-In, *his sister*
Lord Morotaka, *warden of the maids of honour*
Lady Tonase, *his sister*
Lord Moritsugu, *Yoshitsugu's elder brother*
Lord Katsuyori, *Takiguchi's father*
Genjo, *the executioner*
Genkuro } *Outlaws*
Muzo
Kamawake, *six-year-old son of Karumo and Yoshitsugu*
Moon
Titmouse
Kojiju } *maids of honour*
Kohagi
Peasant girl
Servant
Various retainers

Scene One

Night. Mysterious music. Enter the **Moon** *slowly dancing.*

Moon
    I am the beauty of the moon,
    Loved by the sun, and I will soon
    Sing you a love-song not too long,
    Which has been my unchanging song,
    No matter what they say, since time
    Began – the steps of stars I climb
    Are eyes in ecstasy, the full
    Circle I grow to when I pull
    Oceans, is passion; see these scars,
    My beauty has more wounds than Mars,
    But is still beauty. I have died
    More times than Lucifer has lied,
    And vanished utterly – but still
    You keep on climbing, Jack and Jill.

Exit. Day rises. Enter **Titmouse** *dancing.*

    Titmouse
    I woke up in a tiny sky
    So tight on me I could not fly,
    But when I grew my beak it broke,
    And then I think I really woke.
    Out of the sky into the sky –
    If this one breaks as well, goodbye!

Enter a bird catcher, who nets the **Titmouse**. *An arrangement of suspended rings is brought on, and an ornamental well. With a stick the catcher makes the* **Titmouse** *hop through the rings and draw water from the well.*

    Titmouse
    This is a shell my beak can't break,
    A dream from which I cannot wake.
    I knew a cage more cramped than this,
    But after that I had such bliss
    That to be in the shell again
    Is a new universe of pain.

But I have this to sing about —
If I got in I can get out!

Enter **Lord Shigemori**, **Takiguchi**, **Yoshitsugu**,
Moritsugu *and other samurai, who take up positions at attention.*
Enter **Lady Tonase**.

Lady Tonase
Lord Keeper of the Privy Seal, your sister
The empress, has despatched me to inform you
That since in her opinion in the mountains
The maple leaves must now be at their best,
Past as we are the first week of September,
It is her wish that you, Lord Shigemori,
Arrange an expedition to pick mushrooms,
As is our yearly custom, on Mount Kita.

Shigemori
Your message fills me with delight, my lady,
Pre-empting as it does my own intention
To broach this matter with Her Majesty.
Lady Tonase, would you be so kind
As to inform Her Majesty my sister
That we will look for mushrooms on the twelfth,
And on the thirteenth view the moon, as usual;
And to implore her kindly to prolong
By a few days her visit to the mountain,
After the parties.

Lady Tonase   I will do so gladly.
Your invitation fills me with delight,
And I can well imagine what a welcome
The news will meet with from Her Majesty.
The younger — as indeed no less the elder
Ladies-in-waiting such as I look forward
To the two annual Imperial
Picnics with great anticipation always,
The viewing of the flowers in the spring,
The viewing of the maple leaves in autumn.
I must delay no longer, but return
To my Imperial beloved mistress

Your lordship's kindly answer. I can see
That red already, hanging on the trees,
Like heaven's dresses! In the tuneful fields
The insects strum invisible guitars;
And since the weather has been clear, for sure
The beauty of the moon will not be veiled.
My thanks to all your lordship's samurai
For the great pains I know they will be at
To make this expedition a success.
And so I beg to take my leave, your lordship.

Exit.

Shigemori
Good comrades, Yoshitsugu, Takiguchi
And Moritsugu, my best samurai,
You hear the mushroom-picking expedition
Is to be on the twelfth. You must excel
In your attendance, as you always do,
Sweeping the slopes of fallen leaves, erecting
The holiday pavilion, and escorting
Her Majesty the Empress to the mountain.
Further, the special passion of the Empress
Being for songbirds, you are to assemble
A spacious cage in front of the pavilion,
Beautiful, and containing beautiful
Songbirds of all the seasons. And the titmouse
Presented to me by Lord Kadowaki
Recently, can perform, or so they say,
Tricks at suggestions of the hand, for instance
Hopping through rings – it would be childish of me
To keep the jongleur for myself, and therefore
I plan to give it to Her Majesty.
The errand, Takiguchi, shall be yours.
Make yourself ready.

Takiguchi   Happily, my lord.

Exeunt, **Takiguchi** *a different way from the others, carrying the*
Titmouse *in a cage.*

Scene Two

The **Empress***'s palace. The maids of honour,* **Yokobue**,
Karumo *and* **Kohagi***, are playing and gossiping. Enter* **Kojiju**.

Kojiju
Lady Tonase has announced the day!

Kohagi
The mushroom day? When is it? Soon?

Kojiju   Quite soon!

Kohagi
Not soon enough – I want to see the mountain!

Kojiju
Who do you call the mountain?

Karumo   When's the day?

Kojiju
The twelfth.

Yokobue   The twelfth of what?

Kojiju   The twelfth of now.

Kohagi
Next week! Oh God, oh God, that gorgeous mountain!

Kojiju
There will be mountains walking on the mountain.

Kohagi
Our escort! Ah, the shiny maple leaves.

Kojiju
The naked moon!

Karumo   Control yourself, Kojiju.

Kojiju
Oh but Karumo, all the samurai
Are over sixty in this place. Imagine,
Young ones, not withered, not like Morotaka
Sending us endless dog-eared notes of passion.

Yokubue
Don't hope for much. The younger samurai
Aren't so much better.

Kojiju   Yokobue Dono!

Kohagi
Who will Lord Shigemori bring, I wonder.
I only want to be a mountaineer,
To stand on every peak and kiss the sky,
But fate will choose us husbands made in hell
Unless we think ahead.

Kojiju   Oh but the maple!
There will be bad ones and there will be good ones,
It's up to us to choose; a man is perfect
If he attracts me, rubbish if he doesn't.
Who do you choose, Kohagi?

Kohagi   Tunemasa –
Is the most handsome of the Taira men,
Everyone says – and so I thought at first,
For a long time, but then I realised
He's just a boy parading as a man,
Life is a game to him, he's paper thin.
I cannot love a painting of a man,
No matter what a masterpiece it is.
Kojiju?

Kojiju I adore Lord Atsumori –
Oh, he's so stupid! Every time he speaks
It breaks my heart. But men as lovable
As him soon fall; I fear he has been taken.
Karumo?

Karumo I love Yoshitsugu Dono.

Kojiju
We know.

Kohagi Oh very bravely said, Karumo.

Karumo
I cannot comment on his character.

Kohagi
Which is the best description you could give.
I envy you – though Master Morihisa's
Beautiful flute entranced me for a moment,
Because he told me that he is a woman
I had to let him go. Like Tunemasa.
But I have seen perfection in a man,
And it is Takiguchi. Yokobue,
Don't you agree? Be honest, like Karumo!

Yokobue
No! He is just another Tunemasa!
I can see through him! He is handsome, warm,
Honest and kind, but it's a pantomime.

Kojiju
Oh feeble lying echo!

Yokobue   No it's true!
How can he not be vain?

Kojiju   Oh! Tickle her!
Honest Karumo tells us what she feels,
But Yokobue makes excuses!

Kohagi   Pinch her!

Yokobue
Ouch! But I hate him!

Kohagi   Liar! Little liar!
Why did you stitch the seam of his hakama
When it was broken? At the football match,
We saw you kiss it in a tender place
Before you gave it back to him to wear!

Kojiju
You kissed a towel that had wiped his face!

Kohagi
Yet you don't like him!

Kojiju   Dreadful Yokobue!
Confess you do or we'll untie your obi
And strip you to the skin!

Yokobue   Oh please! Forgive me!

Kohagi
Tickle her till she screams!

Yokobue   I am! I'm screaming!

Kohagi
Wise ladies, learn a lesson from this girl's
Horrendous punishment. The search for love
Is serious. The beauty of our bodies
May be surrendered to unworthy men
If we disguise our feelings, and our grace
Will utterly be trampled in the dust.

Enter **Takiguchi** *with the bird to an ante-room separated from the maids by paper doors.*

Takiguchi
Saito Takiguchi, messenger
From the Lord Shigemori, has arrived
To give his message to the lady usher.

Kohagi (*to* **Yokobue**)
What a coincidence! That's you today!

Kojiju
Speak of an angel!

They go to the paper doors and peep through.

Kohagi   Oh those manly cheeks,
I want to bite them! To be in those arms
And to be squeezed and squeezed until I died!

Kojiju
Oh Yokobue, little flute indeed!
That's what your name means. Wouldn't it be nice
For him to lift you to his lips and play!

Kohagi
I'd bring him tea – I'd dust and sweep and clean –

Enter **Lady Tonase**.

Lady Tonase
What is this chattering and foolishness!
Her Majesty has clapped her hands two times,
Yet, brainless girls, not one of you attends her!

Kohagi
That's it, the weather's broken, run for it!

Kojiju
Thunder and lightning!

Kohagi   Wind!

Kojiju   The world is ending!

Exeunt **Lady Tonase, Kohagi, Kojiju, Karumo. Yokobue**
goes to the paper door.

Yokobue
Enter, Sir messenger!

Enter **Takiguchi** *through the paper doors.*

Takiguchi   Lord Shigemori –

Sees it's her and stops.

Yokobue
What is your message?

Takiguchi   I have never, never –

Pulls himself together.

Lord Shigemori orders me to say
That he requests Her Majesty the Empress
To set out early in the morning of
The day after tomorrow for Mount Kita –
I think of you till dawn begins my dreams,
My nights are true, my days are fantasies,
You float before me like the sun on water,
I do my work, I speak and smile, I function,
But your light hands are resting on my mind,
Turning me like the world towards the evening,
When night and quiet cure my brain of fever,

And I awake to think of you again.
Between his birth and death, a warrior
Should not weep once, but if I touch my eyelids
My fingertips are wet. And can you guess
For whom I cry? What nonsense am I talking?
As I was saying, this amazing titmouse,
At a suggestion of the hand draws water
And hops through rings – and we have therefore named it
'The wonder of the capital'.
Lord Shigemori begs to be permitted
To give this titmouse, knowing as he does
That she loves songbirds, to Her Majesty.
But first, my sweetheart, you must entertain
The lady usher with some tricks of yours.

Music. **Takiguchi** *suggests with his hand.* **Titmouse** *hops through the rings and draws water from the well.*

Oh Yokobue Dono, I have made
A little verse about this bird for you.
Poetry is the only trick I know.
Please listen.

    It flies through seven rings
    At a sign.
    Oh lift your spirit's wings
    Through seven lives to be mine!

This is my poem. Would it be too much
To ask you for another in reply?

Yokobue
Dear Takiguchi, it was very sweet.

Thinks.

    The walnut, its desire,
    Can be found
    Where skies of maple fire
    Scarlet shadow the ground.

Takiguchi
And we could meet there at the mushroom hunting,
If that is what your poem means.

Yokobue   Exactly.

Takiguchi
The little valley on Mount Kita –

Yokobue   Yes.

Takiguchi
I will not fail to find you there, I promise.

They draw together and, embracing, upset the cage. The bird flies out.
Yokobue *shrieks. The bird flies around the room.*

Takiguchi
Quick! Get it!

Yokobue   Hush! The others mustn't hear!

Titmouse
To the garden! To the garden!

Takiguchi
Come back!

The **Titmouse** *flies out.*

Yokobue   Oh no!

Takiguchi (*to people off*) You people in the garden!

Re-enter **Titmouse**.

Titmouse
Not the garden! Not the garden!

Yokobue
That's it, come back!

Takiguchi
Please, please, or else we're finished!

Yokobue
You love your little cage!

Titmouse
Yes the garden, yes the garden!

Exit.

Takiguchi   Oh no! Oh no!

Yokobue (*to the people in the garden*)
It's coming back, you people in the garden!

Takiguchi
Ah! Morotaka's there! He's seen! He's coming!

Enter **Morotaka**.

Excellent! Morotaka! You are in charge of security at the
palace, a bird has just escaped, that was a present from Lord
Shigemori —

Morotaka (*staring at* **Yokobue**)
I know about the bird. I see. I see.

Takiguchi
No, this is Yokobue, Morotaka,
She is secure, the bird is in the garden.
And it will soon be in the world, so hurry!

Morotaka
The bird has gone, the damage has been done.
The question now is who to blame, and punish.
Crimes disappear into the past so swiftly,
But retribution stretches to the future.
Why should I run into the garden shouting,
Trying to herd the clouds or gather sunrays,
When here the criminal abides my power,
And something can be done? I have before me
The centre of the chaos — it is spreading
Like ripples from this room. And time is mine
To pierce my reason deep into its cause.

Takiguchi
Do you suggest that —

Morotaka   I do not suggest.
What things suggest to me I state. My duty
Is to protect this place, where every office
Except my own, is in a woman's hands.
I answer to the Empress for them all,

Which is to say, I must account for chaos
Beyond belief to grace above my nature.
A sea of intrigue whispers under me,
And I must keep it decent for the moon.

Takiguchi
If you are daring to accuse this lady —

Morotaka
I think that even in the Emperor's
Palace a certain etiquette inheres
Between an usher and a messenger.
And there they are all males. How much more here,
Where nature hides the seeds of anarchy
In every contact with the outside world,
Is it important to restrain oneself!
Allow a single lapse of concentration
Here, and the upright ladies of the Empress
Are harlots and her palace is a brothel!

Takiguchi
You shall not say this —

Morotaka   So the bird has gone,
Let loose by your surrender to desire,
And we will never get it back again.
I see the cage tipped over, and your face
Flushed. You have failed, and you shall be disgraced.
Young woman, if you were a samurai
Your punishment would be a crushing one,
But you can only suffer as yourself,
And so your sentence is imprisonment.
Prisoner, I must bind your hands behind you!

Takiguchi (*stepping between*)
No, Morotaka Dono, Yokobue
Must not be punished for this accident.
I am to blame entirely, and I shall
Commit seppuku in apology.
But we must understand each other first.
You spoke just now about the punishment
Proper to this offence for samurai.

It was committed by a samurai,
What punishment do you intend for me?

Morotaka
To punish you was not my implication.
If any samurai of mine was guilty
Of such a lapse of duty, I would have him
Bound and beheaded and his head exposed
On the town gates to shame his memory.
Lord Shigemori is your lord, however,
And you are his responsibility.
So roast the titmouse on a spit and eat it,
Pluck it and wear its feathers in your hair,
It's all the same to me. Commit seppuku,
It is your right. But that will not diminish
One bit the punishment of Yokobue.

Yokobue
Ah, Morotaka Dono, you condemn
Others for what you long to do yourself!
Your office is to keep the maids of honour
Chaste and secure, so how can you explain
The love notes you have sent to all of us?

Takiguchi
I must believe the lady. As you said,
A samurai would suffer death for this.
I, a retainer of Lord Shigemori,
Shall carry out the sentence and at once
Bind you, behead you, and expose your head.
Old hypocrite, prepare yourself for death!

Morotaka
You shall not bind me!

They are about to fight. Enter the **Empress**.

Empress (*quietly*)   Let the fighting stop.

Lady Tonase
Her Majesty desires you not to fight!

Takiguchi, Morotaka *step back and bow to the* **Empress**.

Empress
If there was ever proof of misbehaviour
Among my maids of honour, Morotaka,
Their warden, would be blameful. So I think
That Yokobue must be innocent.
That Takiguchi let the bird escape
Is no offence at all. From time to time
He had to feed it and to give it water,
And it should not surprise us that the sky
Calls to the caged one with the claims of freedom,
And when the door was opened out it went.
But it alighted in the inner garden,
And happily as I was passing by
I saw her sitting on a branch and caught her,
And I have put her in the aviary.
I learn that on Mount Kita there will be
A cage of songbirds for my entertainment.
Inform Lord Shigemori, Takiguchi,
That I shall place the titmouse with the others,
And she will sing among them. Yokobue
And Takiguchi, fret no more about her.
Girls, entertain the messenger with sake,
Refresh him. Courage, gentle Takiguchi,
And thank Lord Shigemori heartily
For this most precious present. Morotaka,
It is my strict command that you constrain
All those beneath you to the strictest silence
Upon this matter. If it should be breached,
You will be guilty of a breach of duty.

Exit. Exeunt.

Scene Three

The mountainside, before dawn. Enter **Titmouse** *dancing.*

Titmouse
   Break your cage bird of the sky!
   Shatter the enormous bars

Of darkness riveted with stars,
And spread the wings of day, as I

Have done, escaping to the mountain.
Darkness is breaking. Oh sing praise!
I will hop through rings of days,
Ripples that widen from light's fountain.

But I can see a company,
A striding avenue of pines
With butterflies between the lines,
And they have caged a symphony.

Enter samurai with a large cage containing birds of every shape and colour. They run about and sing conflicting songs frantically. Enter **Shigemori** *and the* **Empress**.

Empress
The mountain air is light, as if the moon
Had worn away to wind one autumn dawn,
It is as if we breathe it through our eyes.
And the bright distance is a memory
Present without an effort of the mind.

Shigemori
But look, the sky has sent us hostages,
And while we keep them gently in our power,
The weather will be fine. The afternoon,
Indulgent to our wishes, is confessing
Its secrets in the language of the dawn.

Empress
But does it sing the same song caged as free?
And though we hear it well, does not its sound
Partly depend on freedom for its tone?
And oh my Lord, I thank you for your kindness
To my delight in showing them to me,
But it would make me even happier,
Having observed them caged, to see them free.
Permit me to release them, and your gift,
That would have faded, will be infinite.

He nods. She lets the birds out. Their songs of confusion turn to joy and they run and dance with the **Titmouse** *and exeunt.*

Shigemori
This was a sacred action. I am trembling,
The gods are here. All grief has disappeared,
And I am staring at a cloudless mountain
I never saw before. Beloved sister,
My ears are open – when the night comes down,
How clear the calling of the deer will be.

Exeunt.

Scene Four

Night on the mountain. Enter **Yoshitsugu** *stealthily, veiled.*

Yoshitsugu (*lifts veil and whispers*)
Karumo! Is it you, my love? Karumo!
No, it's a shrub. The maple roof is thick,
It sieves the precious silver from the air
And lets through only shadows. Oh, Karumo!
She should be here by now – it's Yoshitsugu!

Exit. Enter **Yokobue**, *veiled.*

Yokobue
Oh Takiguchi, this is where the bird
Looks for its food. The Empress didn't catch her,
She said she did, to get us out of trouble.
And I am also free, and here I fly
To seek my lover in the undergrowth.

Enter **Yoshitsugu**, *veiled. They fly into each other's arms, then quickly apart, looking around.* **Yoshitsugu** *gestures and takes* **Yokobue** *on his back. Exeunt. Enter* **Karumo**, *veiled.*

Karumo
According to the angle of the moon,
Midnight has passed. The far deer's cry falls clear
Like snow into a pond, it disappears

Into the stillness; and the fox's cry
Climbs like a flame on paper and is gone.

Enter **Takiguchi** *veiled. They fly into each other's arms and do as the
others. Exeunt. Re-enter* **Yokobue** *and* **Yoshitsugu** *the other way.
Re-enter* **Takiguchi** *and* **Karumo**. *Both couples are unsure if the
other is their reflection. They establish that this is not the case.*

Takiguchi
Hey, Yoshitsugu, is it you?

Yoshitsugu   Indeed!
Can it be Takiguchi?

Takiguchi   Yes it can!

Yoshitsugu
Don't jump, but there's a woman on your back.

Takiguchi
Help, help, it must have fallen from a tree.
You've got one too.

Yoshitsugu   These woods are full of them.

Takiguchi
What are you doing out at night, you devil?

Yoshitsugu
I'm fast asleep in bed.

Takiguchi   But what you're dreaming
Is unforgivable.

Yoshitsugu   The moon's to blame.

Yokobue
Did you say Takiguchi?

Yoshitsugu   Yoshitsugu.

Karumo
Did you say Yoshitsugu?

Takiguchi   Takiguchi.

Karumo
But I'm Karumo.

Yokobue   But I'm Yokobue.

Takiguchi
You took my woman!

Yoshitsugu   Did I really? Sorry!
But you took mine.

Takiguchi   But only from politeness.

Yoshitsugu
It was extremely nice to carry you,
And to imagine that you were my love.

Yokobue
Thank you. So kind of you to carry me.
I'm glad we didn't get where we were going.
Karumo!

Karumo   Yokobue! Are you me?

Yokobue
Almost – apparently –

Takiguchi   Complete disaster
Has been averted by the narrow margin
Of a first name. Farewell, my dears, farewell,
And better luck!

Yoshitsugu   Our love was brief, but true,
Mistaken, but intense.

Takiguchi   Farewell, farewell!

Yoshitsugu
Farewell, my love!

Yokobue   Farewell, lost love, farewell!

Karumo
You never shall be mine, but never mind!

Takiguchi
I'm glad to lose you to this man, farewell!

Exeunt with correct lovers. Enter **Morotaka** *with retainers carrying torches and the butterfly banner.*

Morotaka
The night is silent with the cries of love
Held in by terror, like my conscience,
That may not speak of what has been revealed,
But are prevented by authority
From punishing a clearly proven wrong,
And must pursue it secretly in darkness
To cage it at an even bolder moment.
Two maids of honour are reported missing,
Their names are Yokobue and Karumo.
Their lovers are the kind of samurai
Who think our order is above the law.
Search for them.

Exeunt. Re-enter lovers opposite ways. They stand to either side of the stage, staring into each other's eyes.

Yoshitsugu
This is the place.

Karumo   No one will find us here.

Takiguchi
The ghosts are peaceful here, and they will share
A moment of their after-life with us.

Yokobue
I only hope they're blind.

Takiguchi   No need to worry,
Ghosts only see the feelings, not the actions.

They are invisible in the darkness now, making love.

Yoshitsugu
Karumo!

Karumo
Hush!

Takiguchi
Yokobue!

Yokobue
Hush!

Karumo
Yoshitsugu!

Yoshitsugu
Hush!

Yokobue
Takiguchi!

Takiguchi
Hush!

Karumo
Forever.

Yoshitsugu
Forever.

Yokobue
Forever.

Takiguchi
Forever.

We become aware of lights moving in the distance.

Yoshitsugu
What are those lights descending through the pines?

Takiguchi
Torchlights approaching!

Yoshitsugu　　　　　　　　　And the butterfly!

Karumo
What? Is it Morotaka after us?

Yokobue
He must have searched our rooms!

Takiguchi　　　　　　　　　How rude of him.

Yoshitsugu
How many of them?

Takiguchi   Never mind, too many,
We've got the girls.

Yoshitsugu (*to the girls*)   Could you escape from here,
Across the stream and back to the pavilion?

Karumo
At love's command we could escape through fire.

Takiguchi
We will delay the monster while you run.
My darling, kindly lend me your katsugi.

Yokobue (*giving him her veil*)
Here.

Yoshitsugu   Run away! Good luck!

Karumo   Good luck!

Takiguchi   They're
coming.

Exeunt **Yokobue** *and* **Karumo**. **Takiguchi** *disguises himself as
a woman. Enter* **Morotaka** *and his followers*.

Morotaka
Surround them! So the argument is proved.
Your Majesty, despite your urge to mercy,
You must condemn them now. We must confess
That night has fallen, when the sun goes down,
And when a man lies rotting in the ground,
We must confess that he is dead. So now,
With the plain risen moon of this misdoing,
That smells so foul, we cannot quibble. Veil
The face of your forgiveness for an instant,
My gentle Empress, while impatient justice
Thoroughly cleanses. It is merciful,
Criminals always give themselves away,
They long to broadcast their disgrace, and pain
Forces them slowly out into the open,
More brazen every time they are forgiven,
Vice rises livid where the kiss was planted.
And what my words describe stands proved before us.

Yoshitsugu
What vice stands proved?

Morotaka   The horror of seduction,
You sir, a living wrong. So, Yoshitsugu!

Yoshitsugu
Not so, I only came outside this minute
To see the moonlight on the maple leaves,
I swear I did. And I had no idea
That there was anybody here. Seduction?
My very soul recoils from the suggestion.

Morotaka
Pathetic lie. If you are Yoshitsugu,
This is Karumo. And I recognise her;
How could I not? I am in love with her.
Could I lie dreaming while you ruined her?
Suspicion laid me on a bed of knives,
Sympathy for her unprotected spirit
Stung me with nightmares. Somewhere in the night,
I sensed, dark spirits were devouring her,
Extinguishing her inner light. I leapt
From sleep and rushed instinctively to where
She stood bewitched exactly as I dreamed.

Yoshitsugu
You have a very strong imagination.
But as for love, it cannot be imagined.

Morotaka
Child, I have loved her for two years entirely,
And I intended, if she would permit it,
To ask the Empress to bestow her on me
In legal marriage, not for entertainment.
Now it appears that my incessant efforts
Have been to gather water in a sieve,
Because you had debauched her from the start.
You, a corrupter of the maids of honour,
Prevented me, their warden, from providing
For the security of one of them
Eternally, with love and constancy.

You have seduced my future, and before
We could so much as marry, you have drawn
My darling wife into adultery!
Adulteress!

Rushes at **Takiguchi** *and tears off his veil.*

Takiguchi   Unhand me, frightful man!

Morotaka
What? What? Then – then –

Yoshitsugu   Then then what what, my
friend?

Morotaka
Then Yokobue must be hereabouts.
You saw us coming; like the wolves you are,
Scented the hunters and let fall your prey.
And it has fled. Enough for now, my boys,
The women in this wood are men it seems,
We must proceed by day in this affair.

Makes to leave. **Takiguchi** *blocks his exit.*

Takiguchi
No, no, continue! Justice must be done!
I want to hear your wisdom, Morotaka,
It is so clear, I crave it, give me more,
It is a clever cell, without the window
Of one excuse for evil to climb out of.
And you are your own self's most stern corrector,
That is your greatness. If you should accuse
A samurai, and he was proved not guilty,
You would give satisfaction, I am certain,
And if you should disveil mistakenly
Another, you would not decline his challenge.

Morotaka
Gentlemen, if I have offended you,
I beg forgiveness. You must understand,
I am the herdsman of a flock of vixens,
A fisherman whose nets are made of water.

The difficulty of my duty leads me
Into confusion often. I am certain
That it is Yokobue and Karumo
Who are to blame, and not yourselves. Your honours
Are not my care – they are; my fears for them
Have panicked me into accusing you.
Forgive me, women make us do these things!

Takiguchi
Oh Morotaka, in a castle wall
You are the crack that speaks of standing firm.
Far, far away in heaven where you gaze,
Order is everlasting, but within you,
Fiery chaotic spheres collide forever.
You have condemned yourself again, my friend,
As you will always, till the day you die;
So you have loved Karumo for two years?
Who else but you is her seducer then?
We are two friends out walking in the night.
Prepare to die – as you have said before,
The sentence for this crime is to be bound,
And shamefully beheaded. Yoshitsugu,
I will behead him. Bind him instantly.
And we will also scourge his followers.

Exeunt followers in panic.

Morotaka
You have destroyed me with an argument.
But you are just like that to me – mere words.
And I will follow justice to the end
Against the women whose good name is mine!

Exit.

Takiguchi
Their good name is his?

Yoshitsugu
So they're called Morotaka?

Takiguchi
Yes, we're both in love with Morotaka.

Yoshitsugu
But that's not a very good name.

Takiguchi
Don't blame me, I'm a mere word.

Exeunt.

Scene Five

Katsuyori's *house. Enter* **Katsuyori** *as priest, carrying robes of state.*

Katsuyori
Civil disturbance. In the sea of passion
The rock of state will break the storm of youth.

Enter **Takiguchi**.

Ah Takiguchi. I have called you home
To make a present of these clothes to you.
You are my heir. As such you are to wear them
To represent our house on state occasions.
Lord Shigemori honoured me with them
For a state banquet many years ago,
And in these trappings I received the guests,
All Ministers of State; but I have shed
Courtly considerations, and am bound
Along the mountain road of meditation
For the Pure Land, as you well know. Each day
I worship Buddha for our family,
At our own temple, and I keep myself
Chaste and devote myself to truth by fasting.
But I will stop beside the road a while,
And trouble my serenity to hear
How you are faring in your life at court.
What does Lord Shigemori think of you?

Takiguchi
Dear Father, my abilities are small,
But I have prospered by your influence,

And I stand highest in his Lordship's favour
Of all my comrades. Thus I am inspired
To serve my Lord with all the loyalty
Of which my soul is capable, attending
To all my duties with the utmost care.
Further to this, Her Majesty the Empress
Inclines herself so kindly to me, that
All messages to her are sent by me;
And at the recent picnic on Mount Kita
Often I had the honour to be summoned
Into the presence of Her Majesty
For various errands. And the maids of honour
And my own comrades all esteem me highly.
So I may hope, things being as they are,
The influence and standing of my Lord
Being so great, to be promoted soon.

Katsuyori
Silence! Promoted into hell perhaps!
Are you so innocent as to suppose
That you can brazen out your ignominy
To me as to a faint retired cloud?
The world and I have parted company,
Indeed, but not my family and I,
And I still care about the world in you,
My joy incarnate. Though my spirit's ears
Listen to heaven where its eyes are gazing,
My body is attentive to the weather
When it brings rumours, good or bad, of you.
All else is merely noise, but your affairs
Strike through the music of the spheres; I hear them,
Though I may be in conference with angels;
You are three quarters of my meditation,
And all my dream. So how can you imagine
That I am unaware of your behaviour?
I know that you adore a maid of honour
Named Yokobue – and that your devotion
Caused you to lose the bird Lord Shigemori
Intended as a present to the Empress.

Only the mercy of Her Majesty
Kept you from the severest punishment
When Morotaka caught you. News of this
Reached me the very day of the event,
Splashed ink across the sky – but you, instead
Of taking near-disaster as a warning,
Intensified, stepped up your misdemeanours,
And, at the recent picnic, so I hear,
Disgracefully, in stealth by night, set forward
Further misconduct with the maid of honour.
If noise of this can reach me on my cloud,
Then how much more will it be known below,
Among the crowd? And what is common knowledge
Is knowledge to the highest and the rarest.
His Lordship is the wisest man alive,
And one can scarcely doubt that he disdains you.
Without the shelter of his patronage,
Our house will perish, and I grieve for this.
You are the centre of this dreadful truth,
Its resonance must surely deafen you,
I shall not speak much longer. I have heard
That Yoshitsugu, your companion, also
Had a liaison with a maid of honour.
Karumo is her name, and she is pregnant,
And Moritsugu, Yoshitsugu's brother,
With a pretended illness has confined
Your comrade in his house. If I should follow
This method and imprison you, our line,
Because you are my only son, would end.
Should I allow this house, because of you,
To sink beneath the memory of slaves?
It was my hope that living quietly,
Supported by the pension graciously
Bestowed upon me by his Lordship, I
Could dedicate my final years to prayer,
And that my spirit, full of light, would climb
To the Pure Land in which your mother shines.
But oh, your actions have destroyed my dreams,
And falling you have dragged me out of heaven.

But it is vain to cry against a demon,
I must return to serve Lord Shigemori,
My seven-year ascent from hell is over,
I am a warrior again forever!

He lets his clerical robe fall to the floor, and stands revealed as a samurai.

Takiguchi
Father, I will renounce my love, I swear,
I will forget the past, begin again,
And serve my Lord with all my heart and mind!
Forgive me for my blunders, Father, please!

Katsuyori (*pushes him aside*)
A father can forgive a thousand crimes,
Loving his son, but in the world at large
Forgiveness has a bitter price — too high,
Often impossible to pay. Your Lord
Cannot forgive the chaos you create.
Heaven, farewell, Saito Katsuyori
Has turned again, and he will once more serve
Lord Shigemori as a warrior!

Exit.

Takiguchi
Oh I am hideous and fearful, I
Have fallen like the shadow of a dragon
Between my mother's and my father's souls,
I have destroyed the road to heaven; blind,
Selfishly reaching out for ecstasy,
My arms like mountains rising from the ground
Have carried them apart to distant countries,
Disintegrating heaven. Their love bore
A love that turned against them in the end,
And set a world between the sun and moon.
But I can pray. Could I have lost the world
To gain my own soul? If I am reborn,
My past will die and I will be forgiven
Both by my Lord and by my family.
There is a way! Ha! Why should I be sad?

Life is a dream, but in the lotus flower,
Where we are one, reality begins.

He puts on the clerical robes left by **Katsuyori**, *and exits.*

Scene Six

A room in the palace of the **Empress** *where* **Karumo**, *pregnant, is held. Enter the* **Empress**.

Empress
O my Karumo, they have locked you up,
But like your infant, waiting to be born,
You wait, unknowing, in a loving prison.
I am in disagreement with the law
That would destroy you; I will have the sentence
Altered from death to banishment, I promise.
I wish I could do more. But take this gift:
Its title is The King of Medicines.
It was a present from the Emperor
Of China to our former Emperor,
Now in retirement, and from him to me,
And so to you. It represents the love
Between a mistress and her maid, that reaches
Beyond this world.

Karumo   Wherever I may be,
Your Majesty, this gift will be a charm,
As precious to me as your memory.

Empress
Farewell Karumo, I will not forget you.

Exit. Enter **Morotaka** *another way, with* **Genjo** *the executioner.*

Morotaka
So the real world asserts itself again.
The ship of state, that listed in a storm,
Crushes the rising waves and rights itself.
Dreams are at best a waste, at worst a crime,
It is the world's curse that a rich man's children

Are always dreamers, with no memory,
Who spend his money on their fantasies,
Murderers of their own security.
Tell me my dear, is peace the fruit of dreams,
Is plenty the result of love, is law
The consequence of unrestrained desire?
Order and plenty are the fruits of graft,
The hard-earned harvest of reality,
The state, the nation, they are not a dream.
I am the warden of reality,
Keeping the maids of honour safe from dreams,
Who has a greater right to you than me?
I ask my friend the executioner,
Genjo, the man who trims the nation's dreams.

Genjo
No one.

Morotaka　　The man who put you here is gone,
He is imprisoned in his brother's house,
And he has left you pregnant and disgraced.
Because you are a servant of the Empress,
The punishment you face is very heavy:
But I still care for you. For many years
I have presented you with my petitions;
Ignoring them has led you to disaster,
And so my case is proved. I am your warden,
But I will gladly sacrifice that office
To be your husband, under your command.
I offer you the sanction of the law,
Salvation from the chaos you are in.
Think quickly, girl, before you suddenly
Slip from the present into memory.

Karumo
You speak with so much force.

Morotaka　　　　　　　　　Because I love you –
Not in a dream, but with the fact of power.
You will be taken from this room by me
Or by my friend the executioner,

And your appearance will remain unchanged;
But will it be the beauty of a bride
Or of a flower just about to die?
Love me, my power can transform the heart
While it preserves the face of things unchanged.
A soldier does not change his uniform
When his king dies, but he must change his vow,
And change inside to serve the dead king's son.
And the moon shines on a new infant's eyes
With a new light, although the moon is old.
And so I ask you to remain the same,
But to transfer your loyalty to me,
And in your beauty I will be reborn.

Karumo
Your kindness is a revelation to me.
To learn not only that you do not hate me,
As I deserve, but that you are prepared
To take me as your lady. O my Lord.
What can I say? I have been lost in darkness,
Hunted by wolves of lust. Your understanding
Could wake me from the nightmare of myself.
But Yoshitsugu – will he not be angry?

Morotaka
If he rebels, by the authority
Entrusted to me by the Empress, I
Can puff him into nothing. Marry me,
And he is exiled to the echo-world
Of futile shouting that the law can't hear.
He has no weight, and he will blow away,
As will your fears. Be only happy, girl,
Kill all your feelings but that boundless one,
And exile helpless thinking. As my wife,
Your happiness is guaranteed by law.

Karumo
Shall I arrange for an abortion, sir,
Or would you rather that I had the child?

Morotaka
You are my girl. A secret operation
Would be a danger to your mother-body.
However, I do praise you for your foresight,
The child will be a delicate reminder
Of an unfortunate miscalculation.
But I must make things sweet and easy for you –
If by good luck the infant is a boy,
I will adopt him as my son and heir.

Karumo
Ah, but I fear him. When he comes of age,
And learns that you disposed of Yoshitsugu,
His father, surely he will plan your murder.

Morotaka
Learn what I am. I am a stormy sea,
No man can cross me. I am like a castle
With walls as smooth as ice, unscaleable.
If any man opposes me, he dies.
Let generation after generation
Make me their path to death!

Karumo   Oh Morotaka!
How utterly you steal my heart away
With your sweet talk of murdering my child,
And your kind promise to destroy my lover!
You are not human, your intelligence
Is like the sharpness of a flint, dead stone
That has been shaped for someone else's use.
You breathing statue, can you not imagine
That your great nation had to be imagined
Before it could be made? That peace existed
Before the peace your weapons have created?
Love is the dream from which we take our form,
And you would have me take a form of stone,
Dreamless as death, as constant as a cliff.
The dream whose shape I hope for is not that.

Morotaka
Then you shall die and take a corpse's shape.

For just that purpose – take the girl away
To Funaoka-Yama. Kill her there.

Karumo

You cannot take my life, my punishment
Is banishment, Her Majesty has promised.

Morotaka

The sentence for the crime you have committed
Is death. We know that if I take the trouble
To ask the Empress, she will soften it
To banishment, but if I act in haste
It is the letter of the law I follow
Not my own will – I would be criticised,
But only for my over-diligence.
Genjo has no objections, and he knows
The etiquette of execution well.

Karumo

So I will die if I do not submit
To marry you, and you will execute me
Against the wishes of Her Majesty?
You are a soul more evil than disease!
If Buddha and the gods had taken from me
The light of consciousness that turns within me,
Then I would be your lawful wedded husk.
But as it is I am prepared to die
In generation after generation
Opposing you. So have your fill of murder,
My only terror is for Yoshitsugu,
Trapped in your power. I myself declare
Infinite war. You may destroy my body,
But I will hunt you through a thousand lives
Until as many deaths have worn you down
Into the form and spirit of a worm!

Morotaka

Genjo! This woman's sentence is pronounced.
Take her away to Funaoka-Yama;
And there do with her what I said before.

Genjo *exits with* **Karumo**.

Scene Seven

The cemetery of Funaoka-Yama. Evening. Funeral fires. Enter
Takiguchi *as priest, with a bell around his neck which he strikes*
with a stick. He chants, then speaks.

Takiguchi
    Not so easy
    To turn a girl into a prayer,
    To lose my memory
    For a lotus flower.

    Oh she was the kiss
    Of the entire south
    Pressing warm skies
    On the mouth of the north.

    I pray at Ojoin
    Far from the city.
    But I must go to Koyasan,
    Further away.

    As smoke flies
    Out of fires
    Into the sky's
    Great cloud flowers.

To cut my spirit from my place of birth,
I make the sharp bell cry. It is the sound
Of my youth dying. Since my father failed,
I must continue with his pilgrimage.
He failed because of me, but I have heard
That once Mongaku took the lotus road
Because of love, and by his dedication
Led to the Pure Land everyone he loved.
Oh Yokobue do not think of me,
But send your mind into the lotus flower;
We must forget the world and one another
To be together there; two minds, one image,
That is two rivers flowing to the sea.
I make my way around the cemeteries
To mingle with the spirits of the dead,

And here I am at Funaoka-Yama,
For the last time. It is too near the city,
From which the ripple-spreading breath of rumour
Breaks the reflection of the face of heaven.
I am imperfect here. Oh Mother, Father!
The vague smoke staggers from the funeral pyres.
Namu Amida Buddha, by your mercy
May everything that lives attain your nature.

Enter **Genjo***, followers and* **Karumo** *bound.*

Genjo
Shame that such beauty should be thrown away,
Like a rejected sketch, not good enough.
Marry my master, lady, reconsider!

Karumo
I am already far away from here.
If I dismissed your master's argument,
How will the echoes of his slave convince me,
Faint wind-blown shadow of a ragged scarecrow?
Despatch me to the land beyond your odour.

Genjo
Well if she will not bend she must be broken.

Lifts his sword and takes his station behind her. He is about to strike
when **Takiguchi** *rushes forward and shields her.*

Takiguchi
Wait, sir!

Genjo   Oh! Priest! Get back! Get out of it!
Pleading is useless, she has been condemned.

Takiguchi
Of course she has – that's not what I intend.
You are about to execute this woman
For a grave crime, and she deserves the sentence,
I do not doubt it – sin must be rewarded –
But she is pregnant; for as many months
As it has lived on earth, the child inside her
Will have so many patron gods and Buddhas.

Queen Maya's scripture tells us that these patrons
Of murdered infants fall upon the killer
With sudden death before the year is out,
Either through sickness or by violence.
Nevertheless, suppose a warrior
Must kill a pregnant woman. To avert
The fury of the guardians in this case,
He must repeat a sacred formula
Three times before he carries out the action.

Genjo
Can this be true? I never dreamed of it!
Priest, thank you, you have saved a soul today!
And since you have, would it be possible,
Out of your charity, to ease my duty
By teaching me the sacred formula?

Takiguchi
In order to attain it I endured
Severe austerities for twenty days,
It is my most prized secret; but your life
Depends on knowing it. I would be wrong
To murder by unwillingness to teach.
But you must never tell it to another.

He shoos the others away and says the formula to **Genjo**.

Riken Sokuze Midago.

Genjo
Riken Sokuze Midago.

Takiguchi
Issho Shonen Zaikaijo.

Genjo
Issho Shonen Zaikaijo.

Takiguchi
Now say it quickly three times.

Genjo
Riken Sokuze Midago –

Takiguchi
No, no, no – Riken Riken Riken –

Genjo
Riken Riken Riken, Sokuze, Sokuze –

Takiguchi
No, no, no! Riken, Riken, Riken, Sokuze Midago, three
times –

Genjo   Riken Riken Riken, Sokuze Midago, Sokuze
Midago –

Takiguchi   No! No!

Genjo
What? This is far too difficult for me.
Haven't you got another formula,
One word to say once?

Takiguchi   Slight intelligence
Is all it needs – but you can still be saved –
I will recite the magic formula
Over your sword, which will enchant the blade,
And separate you from its sacrilege.
Give me the sword.

Genjo   You are extremely kind.
Charm it, and take away the blame from it.

Gives the sword to **Takiguchi**.

Takiguchi
Well done, well done, this is the quickest way
To be forgiven, not to do the crime!

Genjo
This was a trick to get my sword! Imposter!
False priest! Return it to me instantly
Or you will die. Are you a lunatic?
Why lose your life to save a criminal?

He springs at **Takiguchi**, *who steps aside*.

Takiguchi
Now taste the sharpness of Amido's sword!

Genjo
Pathetic priest!

Genjo *is forced to hide behind a large tombstone. His followers fight*
Takiguchi, *who presses them back against the stone. It topples on*
Genjo *and he is killed. His followers flee in dismay.*

Takiguchi
Karumo Dono, do you recognise me?

Karumo
Can I believe it? Is it Takiguchi?
I would be sprawling on the ground by now,
Without a head, if it was not for you!
But why are you a priest?

Takiguchi   I will explain
When there is time. We must escape from here!

Exeunt.

Scene Eight

Enter **Katsuyori** *and* **Moritsugu** *from opposite sides. They bow.*
Moritsugu *sits down.* **Katsuyori** *moves his mat one level up on the*
dais and sits above **Moritsugu**. **Moritsugu** *instantly stands.*

Moritsugu
Look at me closely. I am Moritsugu,
And you have blundered, you should sit below me.

Katsuyori
I recognise you – that is not the problem.
My old eyes see regretfully but clearly.
Memory is the present in decay,
But yours is fading faster than it might;
Nevertheless, please struggle to remember
That you are of the Fifth Grade in court rank,
And I am of the Fourth. Brief calculation
Will show you that the highest seat is mine.
Perhaps you are unwell, and should remain
In your own dwelling, taking medicine.

Moritsugu
Absurd old man! If you do not descend
From this position, I will kick you down –

He manhandles him but then desists.

Which would be dreadful; if your hat fell off
We would behold a bald head.

Katsuyori   Must you mock me?
And must you seize my flesh and, shaking me,
Rattle the fragile skeleton within?
These are the arguments of anarchy,
There is no code of conduct in the world
That will command a Fourth Grade samurai
To sit below a Fifth Grade samurai,
Which you have proved by your resort to force.
Or tell me what is your authority?
Try reasoning, come, argue with me, boy!

Moritsugu
The aimless raging of your mind is proof
Beyond debate of your senility!
Oh sweet almighty and sublime Fourth Grade!
Of which you are a member, I confess;
However, having taken holy vows,
You are ungraded in our hierarchy,
Beside the point, disused and out of office.
And it is Takiguchi's turn today
To be on duty in this drawing-room,
But I have heard that he cannot be found,
But that escaping from his reputation,
He has forsaken the imperfect world,
And gone to hide his shame in sanctimony!
Thanks be for that! Had he remained in office,
The taint of his behaviour might have ruined
Any young samurai who followed him.
Yet he has not escaped – his punishment
Turns on the conscience of Lord Shigemori,
And whether Takiguchi shall be ordered
To kill himself, or will be executed,

Is not yet known. It seems that you, presuming
That your son's vows remove your shame in him,
Have seized the time to serve your Lord again.
This is your second service, and I meet you
For the first time in this capacity;
The order of our duties is unchanged,
And it is Takiguchi's turn today;
I therefore charge you, as his substitute,
To sit below me – I am Moritsugu
Of the Fifth Grade, and you are Takiguchi
Of the Sixth Grade; if I am wrong, correct me.

Places his mat on the second level of the dais.

Katsuyori
So! No more talk of where to place our mats,
Ice-thin excuse for our true argument;
You charge me that my son took holy orders
In order to escape from punishment.
But then you say that to forsake the world
Does not exempt a sinner from the law.
As for your brother, the pretended illness
With which you shelter him from shame at home
I diagnose as this: your cowardice!
It is a public secret anyway.
And it is better for the public good
That Yoshitsugu should be kept apart,
His influence on other samurai
Would swiftly cause a general collapse!
Yet you accuse me, as the scarlet ape
Laughs at the face of Buddha, so they say!

He places his mat on the highest level of the dais.

Moritsugu (*removes* **Katsuyori**'*s mat, places his own on the
highest level*)
Yes, and the sideways-creeping crab is always
Sniggering at the man who walks straight forwards!

Katsuyori (*removes* **Moritsugu**'*s mat, puts his own in its place*)
Ah, but the daisy on the ground is right
To mock the poppy in the magpie's beak!

Moritsugu (*swaps the mats again*)
Yes, but the man crucified upside down
Dies laughing at the head upon a pole
Kissing his feet.

Katsuyori   As you yourself will prove!

Moritsugu
Are you familiar with the taste of steel?
Then I will show you –

Katsuyori   If you think you can!

Moritsugu
I will oblige you now if you desire!

They are about to fight. Enter **Lord Shigemori** *and sits on the top level of the dais. All kneel to him.*

Shigemori
Gentlemen, what good weather we are having.

Enter **Morotaka** *in a hurry.*

Morotaka
Lord Morotaka, with a message for
Lord Shigemori from Her Majesty.
I beg to speak my message to your Lordship.

Shigemori
Speak, Lord Morotaka.

Morotaka
Chaos! And ruptures in the name of love,
Convulsing in the body of the state!
The head is silent in a sacred rapture,
But the limbs quiver and internal bleeding
Threatens the organs. We have given rein
To fragmentation – we were once as one,
But multiplying we have lost our children;
Uncountable, and unaccountable,
They feast on freedom; when we gave it to them,
That day we gave away our unity!

Shigemori
Is this a general account of things,
Or do you have a message to deliver?

Morotaka
My Lord, I have a message. Two court ladies,
Whose names are Yokobue and Karumo,
Recently fell from grace with Takiguchi
And Yoshitsugu. This has been a scandal
That has created discontent at court!
Her Majesty, on learning that Karumo
Was pregnant, so resented the betrayal
This represented, that she ordered me
To have the girl beheaded. To refuse
Was not an option, and despite myself,
I sent the girl to Funaoka-Yama
For execution. As the sword-blade fell,
A stranger out of nowhere suddenly
Attacked and killed the executioner,
My own retainer, Iwamura Genjo,
And carried off the girl. The criminal
Can only be her lover Yoshitsugu;
His evil act of well-planned anarchy
By which the power of the state is blunted
At its effective point, deranged, perverted,
Made to rebound like spitting in the wind,
Left as a specious and unacted word,
Waiting for meaning, this insane reversal,
This farce by which the executioner,
The definition of the state, is murdered
Attempting to enact a state decision,
This sin has so incensed Her Majesty
That she commands the instant execution
Of Yoshitsugu to restore the balance.
The fallen maid of honour Yokobue
Shall be beheaded at the other court.
Her Majesty will give your Lordship notice
Of the arrangements at a later time.
It is the pleasure of Her Majesty

That Yoshitsugu shall be executed
At once, but with the proper ceremony.
This is my message.

Shigemori   Unacceptable.
Unprecedented. There are many cases
Where maids of honour who have taken lovers
Have been forgiven for their indiscretion.
Conscience referring to these precedents
Cannot but find Her Majesty's decision
Excessively severe. Did not your sister
Lady Tonase and yourself join forces
In remonstrating with Her Majesty,
Lord Morotaka?

Morotaka   Yes my Lord, we did,
Time and again my sister and myself,
Like waves and rain both crying on the shore,
Implored the Empress, but it did no good.
Your Lordship's military upbringing
Is also hers, and her decisions echo
The customs of the military classes.

Shigemori
Not so. Her actions are Imperial.
As you describe them, they observe a code
Contrary to the military one.
Your follower, the executioner
Genjo, ignored the military custom
In his arrangements for the transportation
Of the condemned to Funaoka-Yama.
A well-armed escort guards a prisoner
To death with weapons drawn. And this procedure
Is not intended as a luxury,
Protection for a man about to die,
It is designed against the family
And friends of the condemned, who may attempt
Violent rescue. By his negligence
Your follower has thrown away his life,
And, more importantly, his prisoner.

The family of such a warrior,
If he was bound by military law,
Would suffer dearly for his crime. His corpse
Would certainly be crucified. His Lord –
You in this case – would certainly be ordered
To kill himself. The order of the Empress
Follows the customs neither of the court
Nor of the camp, nor of humanity.
And yet the pleasure of Her Majesty
Is in effect the Emperor's command.
And Yoshitsugu shall be executed
Today. Lord Moritsugu, fetch your brother!

Exit **Moritsugu**.

So Yokobue is to be beheaded
At court, Lord Morotaka? I am worried;
Who is to be her executioner?
Genjo the blunderer is dead – and yet,
If Yokobue was to disappear
Out of your keeping as Karumo did,
There would be more than discontent at court.
Therefore you will inform Her Majesty
That I shall send an executioner
And an inspector of my own to her.
This is the answer of Lord Shigemori
To the Imperial command. And yet –
There is another matter; I have heard
A rumour that there is a samurai –
His name so far eludes us – who is working
Destruction on a lady and her lover.
Let it be known that this has been discovered;
And if he does not voluntarily
Submit himself to you for punishment,
Inform me, Morotaka. Understand
That I intend to crush him utterly.

Morotaka
Indeed, of course, no, yes, of course, my Lord!

Exit stumbling and terrified. Enter **Moritsugu** *and* **Yoshitsugu**.

Shigemori
Ah, Yoshitsugu! Please remove your swords.

Yoshitsugu
At once, my Lord.

As he does so, the samurai sigh. They bow their heads and weep silently.

Shigemori
It was the answer of a samurai,
Who cannot speak in any other way,
Even in his reply to the command
To be a samurai no more. Observe him.
He understands, a samurai is nothing
If he does not obey his Lord's command
Even when it commands him to be nothing.
See the perfection of obedience,
Dutiful as an iris to the light,
Rising and dying at the sun's command.
Respect him as you do the rising sun;
True servant and commander of the day,
He steps unstained from the defeat of night,
Armoured in light, and for a while displays
The glamour and the flash of victory,
Whirling his many golden blades, but soon
He runs again into the enemy,
Darkness, whose shadows cover him till dawn.
Remember this perfected samurai,
Remember him. The everlasting stars
Wheeling by troops across the universe
Are not more precious in our memory.
Eternal companies of trees and mountains
Will guard the mound in which we lay our comrade.
Ah Yoshitsugu, I would offer you
The means of death a samurai prefers
To execution, if the choice were mine,
But by the order of Her Majesty
You are to be beheaded. Yoshitsugu,
Do not despair, your never-failing service

Shall be rewarded. It is not my wish
For common hands to execute my friend.
These hands shall do it, and preserve your name,
Conferring no dishonour with the blow.
A good retainer is his Lord's beloved,
We are connected in eternity,
Fighting in one another's cause forever,
It is my head I sever. Yoshitsugu,
Part from your broken-hearted comrades now,
And from your brother with a brief farewell.
I shall await you in the inner courtyard.

Exit.

Yoshitsugu

My brother and my comrades, listen to me.
I feel the shame for which I have to die,
I bless the sentence, I agree with it,
And yet consider this: my Lord has set
A diamond of his wisdom in my darkness,
That has transformed my nothingness to brilliance.
It is as if a blind man, lost at night,
Saw a dim star, and then a shape of stars,
And then the whole sky like a forest fire,
Curved boughs of bristling light, and leaves of flame,
Brighter to him that instant than midday.
My Lord has frightened my disgrace away
With his fierce kindness. And to me the night,
And to be lost – I mean my death, my shame,
Are fiery figures laughing in the sky,
Because my Lord has spoken well of me.
Remember this, my fellow samurai,
My only sorrow is to leave a Lord
Whose word can change defeat to victory;
A man whose wisdom changes death to love.
Oh to be lying in a heap of corpses
Slaughtered in his defence; my death is useless
Compared to that; but if the light it sheds
Reveals the glory of your Lord more clearly,

It had a purpose. So farewell, farewell,
Comrades in honour and my most dear brother.

Exit.

Moritsugu (*in tears*)
I am a happy man! Had Yoshitsugu
Turned to religion, he would not have heard
Such praises from his Lord before he died.
And rather than the privilege of ending
At his Lord's hands, he would have had to bow
His shaven head before a common soldier.
Those who forsake their station die dishonoured,
But Yoshitsugu was a samurai!

Enter **Lord Shigemori** *with two headboxes.*

Shigemori (*to* **Katsuyori**)
I have beheaded Yoshitsugu
And placed the head in this sealed box. Your orders
Are to convey it safely to the court;
There break the seal, and when you have inspected
The head, display it to Her Majesty.
Having done this, you are to execute
The Lady Yokobue. Place her head
In this box, seal it, and return with it.
Your orders, Moritsugu, are to act
As the inspector at her execution.
You must proceed with this immediately.

Katsuyori
I shall obey my Lord without delay.

Moritsugu
You will inspect the head of Yoshitsugu,
And execute the Lady Yokobue?

Katsuyori
Of course. Why not? Will you refuse to act
As the inspector at her execution?

Moritsugu
No, I most certainly will not refuse.

And let me tell you that if your inspection
Of Yoshitsugu's head in any way
Departs from custom – if your execution
Of Yokobue is at all in error,
I shall report it. Do you understand me?

Katsuyori
I do. But understand me perfectly.
If your inspection of the execution
Is in the slightest way irregular,
I shall report that.

Moritsugu   We have heard each other.
Remember that our solemn word was given.
Come then.

Katsuyori Lead on, lead on, where I can see you.

Exeunt **Katsuyori** *and* **Moritsugu** *with the headboxes.*

Scene Nine

The **Empress***'s palace. The* **Empress** *and her ladies,*
Yokobue, Kojiju *and* **Kohagi**.

Empress
The daughters of the winter, hail and rain,
Flap like an ancient wedding dress, gone grey,
Capering gravely on the washing line.
We could resist the negative opinions
Of our old clothes; but the chrysanthemums
Have fallen to the lawn, and the blind garden
Is an old woman naked in her room,
Shuddering like a cobweb in a draft.

Kojiju
Your Majesty, why don't we play hentsugi?

Empress
Far too intense.

Kohagi   Why don't we go outside,
Majesty, for a game of kaiawase?

Empress
Too cold; we need a game that will remind us
Of spring, it's true, but the unhelpful weather
Will not pretend. Aha, I have it though!
Poem cards!

Kojiju   Yes!

Kohagi   Exactly what we need!

Empress
Scatter the cards.

They scatter the cards and chatter excitedly.

Empress (*aside to* **Yokobue**)   Unlucky Yokobue,
This weather is inside you, and your sorrow
Fills the whole sky; the walls protect our bodies,
But you are an enormous open window
Through which the bad wind blows; its battering
Ruins your rooms, and its incessant tugging
Makes rubbish of your hopes, whose scarlet shapes
Hung on the trees like medals. Oh my friend,
You can and will be spring again, I promise,
Depend on me. My friends, I have decided
To be the reader, not to play this time;
But this is my idea – if you consider
The game as divination, and interpret
Each card you pick as speaking for your future,
Then you will find it much more fascinating.
Agreed?

Kohagi   Agreed!

Kojiju   Agreed!

Empress   And Yokobue?
Sit next to me, and since I am the reader,
Who knows, perhaps I can improve your future!
Ready? But since the game in our new version
Is more significant, in my opinion
We should petition for auspicious cards
In silence to the gods of poetry.

A moment of silence. Reads –

> Strangers from unknown lands,
> Friends who have travelled a mile –

Quick, Yokobue, you must get this card.

Yokobue
Thank you, Your Majesty, I must indeed,
I know this one, it speaks about reunion.

Kojiju (*finding the card*)
> Meet at this mountain stile,
> Smile and shake hands.

Empress
Oh, Yokobue! But well done, Kojiju.

> Love has cut me like the scree
> Where the mountain climber slides –

Kohagi (*finding the card*)
> But the cloud above me hides
> My lady, and she does not see.

Poor mountaineer! But he does not mean me,
Nobody pines for me!

Kojiju (*laughing*)   I'm not so sure!

Empress
> Now the double cherry trees
> That grew in Nara long ago –

Now, Yokobue, this is meant for you,
This poem is a message of good fortune.

Kojiju (*finding it*)
> Grow here, and our breezes blow
> The fragrance of their memories.

This is good luck! According to this poem
The dresses I will get as year's end presents
Will be as lovely as the cherry blossom.

Empress
Interpretation taken – somewhat strained,
But it may be your future.

> Feasting on what was said,
> We feed our misery,

Yokobue
Ah! I can see it. It must be for me!

She finds it.

> My husband's love is dead,
> This is the day that I die.

Empress
Do not despair.

> Through nights as long as rain,
> Eroding worlds of stone –

Yokobue (*finding the card*)   I have it!

> I pray for love in vain,
> Eternally alone!

No more!

Empress   You gods of poetry be kind!

> I live alone and free,
> I never speak a word –

I will read this one, I cannot be harmed –

> Yet I am seen and heard
> Under the mountain cherry tree.

Oh Yokobue, never feel alone!
Remember that you have a friend in me,
As strong if not as silent as the cherry.
More poetry!

> As the mountain pheasant's tail,
> Weighed by its length curves down in flight,

Kohagi (*finding card*)
>So this long loneliness of night
>Weighs on me and my strong wings fail.

Empress
Be glad, Kohagi, I will not allow you
To suffer for as long as that, I promise.
Maybe a wagtail's length of loneliness.

>I shall not see another day,
>Her light withdraws and my hope fades,

Kojiju has it – bravely read it out!

Kojiju
>The sun has set, it would not stay,
>For all my prayers and my parades.

Empress
You are fourteen, my darling, and I pray
That you have not yet found yourself exclaiming,
I shall not see another day!

>When I see the King of Frost
>Flash across the magpie bridge,

Kohagi
That's it! I have it! It's a lucky one!

>Then I know that night has lost
>The battle for the eastern ridge.

Heaven, imagine being up so early!

Empress
Poets do not sleep.

>Though a rock divides the river
>Into streams that rush apart,

I think this poem is extremely strong.
The second half is this, if I remember –

>They will join again forever
>In the sea's unbroken heart.

Look, Yokobue, can you see it? There!

Yokobue *scrambles for it and gets it.*

Yokobue
I have it! Thank you!

Empress   Lucky Yokobue!

Yokobue (*reads*)
    Though a rock divides the river
    Into streams that rush apart,
    They will join again forever
    In the sea's unbroken heart.

Enter **Lady Tonase**.

Lady Tonase
Your Majesty, I beg to give my message.
Lord Morotaka will be present shortly
On urgent business that he says requires
The honour of a meeting with the Empress.

Empress
Will he indeed? And could he not present
His news as is the custom through yourself,
Lady Tonase? What can be the matter?
So let him storm us with his urgency.

Lady Tonase
Lord Morotaka!

Enter **Morotaka** *in pretended dejection*.

Morotaka
Greetings on this cold day, Your Majesty!
I am the wind, I groan, Your Majesty,
Under foul news as heavy as this weather,
Too much for me to bear. His Excellency
Lord Shigemori, hearing that Karumo
Had been discharged because her pregnancy
Confessed a love affair, has executed
With his own hands, her lover Yoshitsugu.
And he has sent the head with Katsuyori,
Who will display it to Your Majestry.
The messenger awaits you with his burden.

Further, Lord Shigemori sends this message:
That he believes it right that Takiguchi
Should also lose his life. But Takiguchi
Cannot be found, because he has forsaken
The world. Lord Shigemori thus considers
That Yokobue should be executed
In place of Takiguchi. 'If the Empress
Refuses to surrender Yokobue,
Your duty is to seek out Takiguchi,
And part him from his head.' This was the order
Lord Shigemori gave to Katsuyori.
'But try your utmost to persuade the Empress
To give you Yokobue – if she will,
Behead the girl and bring her head to me.'
These punishments are rash in my opinion,
Unworthy of His gentle Excellency,
But we are weak and it must be. May I
Regretfully suggest the wisest course,
Your Majesty? Do not resist, permit
The executioner to do his duty
On Yokobue. It is very sad,
She served Your Majesty so faithfully!

He weeps.

Empress
I hate to have to speak against my brother,
But it appears that he has lost his mind.
Unmarried passion is indeed a sin,
That Sakya Muni counsels us against,
But love must be allowed to bud; without it
Life is a duty, beauty is a lie.
In poetry's religion love is god;
Courts take their cue from poets. In the past
Even our military rulers often
Forgave court lovers, so my Lord's decision
Breaks with traditions of all kinds, all classes.
Even if it did not, can you imagine
That I would let you slaughter Yokobue,
My servant who has served me faithfully,

Mo matter what her crime? We are connected
By our relationship as maid and mistress
Through three existences, and I will never
Suffer her to be led to execution,
Even if I must lose in her defence
My rank as Empress and my very life.
From this day on forever, Morotaka,
Consider me her sister or her mother.
I will defend my daughter like a tiger,
No one will ever execute my sister.
If you can understand, show mercy, speak
Against this sentence to Lord Shigemori.

Morotaka
I understand your love, but like the wind
I canot change the season; and I fear
That the inspector waiting by the gate,
And the impatient executioner,
Will not be happy to be sent away.
Shall I inform them that the execution
Of Yokobue is impossible,
And that they must depart and by default
Seek out and bring to justice Takiguchi?

Empress
I understand. It is Lord Shigemori's
Steadfast intent that either Takiguchi
Or Yokobue shall be executed.
You tell me that the executioner
And the inspector are already here.
We shall address them. Hurry, girls, and call
The samurai into this private chamber.
You are to hear me also, Morotaka.

Enter **Katsuyori** *and* **Moritsugu** *the other side.*

Kojiju
Lord Katsuyori and Lord Moritsugu.

Empress
Welcome to both of you. Lord Shigemori,
Your Lord, is my respected elder brother.

And he is even more exalted, keeper
Of the Imperial almighty seal.
Yet he has executed Yoshitsugu
With his own hands. My brother is my subject,
I am his master's wife, and I feel able
To state my view that he has lost his reason.
Is it a matter of routine to send
Persons of deathly office to the court?
To desecrate the palace of the Empress
With blood, is that an everyday procedure?
How can I suffer gentle Yokobue,
Who has been with me since she was a child,
To bow in terror to the bitter sword?
No, she will not, although she has to die.
I am a woman, but my family
Are so-called 'People of the bow and arrow' —
I am the sister of Lord Shigemori!
I have not learnt to deal out death in battle,
But I could certainly perform the office
Of execution. And I claim as mine
The duty of beheading Yokobue.
I will display her head to the inspector —
Your name is Moritsugu isn't it?
When I have executed Yokobue,
I will inspect the head of Yoshitsugu.
Daughter, step forward. What is in my power
To save you I have done, but it is nothing.
Therefore prepare to die, my most dear sister.

Yokobue
Most gracious Majesty, your kindness reaches
Above Mount Shumi and below the ocean,
And changes death to friendship. But to stain
With my vile blood your tender honoured hands,
That cannot be! The fury of the heavens
Would make me hateful in my next existence;
I beg one last request, Your Majesty;
Of your benevolence forsake me, leave me
To the appointed executioner.

Since it must happen, I do not complain
About the matter of my execution,
No matter how severe. My hopes are strong
To see my lover in another life.
The only sorrow of my body's death
Is that it parts me from Your Majesty;
To know that even if I should return
Into the earth's existence seven times,
I would not find a mistress of such grace,
Will be my body's only agony.
And so I plead, beloved mistress, leave
His duty to the executioner.

Empress
No, Yokobue, I cannot permit
A samurai to kill my dearest maid.
Settle your fearful mind that it will be
My sword that kills you or no other one.

Takes her sword from the rack, tucks up her skirts.

So come with me, my girl, my sister; death
Waits for you in another room, alone.

Exeunt **Yokobue** *and the* **Empress**. **Morotaka** *stands with face upraised.* **Moritsugu** *and* **Katsuyori** *stare at each other, shocked.*

Moritsugu
O Katsuyori, I am most confused.
Is it not strange to see Her Majesty
Surprised and shaken by her own command?
Lord Shigemori and Her Majesty
Have never disagreed before. Their minds,
Formed in one womb, have followed one another
Since then, like clock hands or like compliments.
Yet suddenly the actions of the one
Are the extreme of horror to the other.
It is as if one saw a devil staring
Back at one from an old familiar mirror.
This is extremely strange.

Katsuyori   In my opinion
There is indeed a devil in the mirror
Of this affair, some human-seeming demon,
Whose motivation is the love of power,
Or love untempered by respect, like sunlight
That smiles through water but can burn through air.
Our squabble was a gentlemanly matter,
But there is danger when Her Majesty
Deplores Lord Shigemori, and he her.
This strikes the state at its most vital joint,
Where love alone preserves our unity.

Moritsugu

Love is so strong that through its influence
A girl can bear the founder of a city,
So weak that it can turn without a warning
Into its opposite, and overnight
Plough its own castles into plains of hatred.
If we two trained and seasoned samurai,
Serving one Lord, can suddenly be changed
Into two children throwing words like stones,
Imagine how unsafe a nation is,
Containing madmen, fools, rejected lovers,
Soldiers with leisure, children with no fathers,
Possessive husbands and uncaring landlords,
Thieves, killers, little kings, the rich, the vain,
All constantly provoking one another.
And yet the only hope of unity
For this unquiet company is love.

Katsuyori

Heaven preserve us. If our leaders argue,
Who will restrict the common people? Safety
Craves chaos, chaos craves in vain for safety,
Everything rushes to its opposite.

Moritsugu

But wisdom can prevent it. We must find
The man of sinful inspiration working
Among us for the furtherance of mayhem,

Provoked by jealousy in love perhaps,
To try to wreck and rearrange the nation
As an arena for his heart's desires;
Perhaps inspired by that severe emotion,
Pure love of power for itself alone.
Whatever this disordered creature's ends,
Disorder is his means; and we must find him,
And drive his spirit to the underworld.

Katsuyori
Destroy his body.

Moritsugu   Rend it utterly.

Katsuyori
Spatter the furrows with his blood.

Moritsugu   Disperse
His fragments to the wind in carrion.
Lord Morotaka, you appear unwell.

Morotaka *started aloof, but as these speeches progress he becomes uneasy, then starts to shudder. Now he is shaking uncontrollably.*

Morotaka
Do I?

Moritsugu   Indeed you do.

Morotaka   But I feel fine.

He convulses violently.

What is the matter? It is just the cold
Making me shiver. I must find a fire –

He trembles all over and can hardly stand.

My friends, forgive my loss of self-control,
It is so cold. To think a samurai
Could feel the cold so badly! Very strange!
And I am sweating – am I feverish?
Are you not cold? I have to find a fire –
Excuse me, noble colleagues, please excuse me –

He can hardly walk but staggers out bent over to one side, shuddering; falls, gets up, exits.

Moritsugu
Lord Morotaka is the warden here,
And we are under his authority.
Odd that he should abandon his position
In an apparent loss of confidence.

Katsuyori
Could it be guilt?

Moritsugu   We must remain observant.

Enter **Lady Tonase** *with the headboxes.*

Lady Tonase
Good evening, sirs. Her Majesty the Empress
Has executed Yokobue.
This box, which, as you see, Her Majesty
Has sealed, contains the head of Yokobue.
My orders from Her gracious Majesty
Are to receive the head of Yoshitsugu
From you, and having done so, to deliver
Into your hands the head of Yokobue.

Katsuyori *bows and unseals his box and removes the lid. They are amazed.*

Lady Tonase
It is a stone – and not his head, his queue.

Lady Tonase *unseals and opens the other box.*

Moritsugu
A flute that has been cut in half – and earth!

Katsuyori (*in wonder*)
I see – I see – oh, I am like a child
Who for the first time hears his parents' words
As more than sounds connected to their mouths.
And how can I refrain from praising them?
Though separate, without a messenger,
Lord Shigemori and Her Majesty
Have carried out one plan. Lord Shigemori

Spared Yoshitsugu's life, and by removing
His queue, created him a priest. The priesthood
Severs a man from what we call the world,
This piece of stone is Yoshitsugu's tomb,
And we can say with truth that Yoshitsugu
Was executed by Lord Shigemori.
Whatever evil Yoshitsugu did,
Died when this queue was severed; just as Buddha
Taught us to say, the bad and good were saved
In the same hour. And look, the same solution:
Her name means flute, and here is Yokobue,
Broken and buried in a little earth.
This symbol signifies that Yokobue
Has been dismissed from court, and in a sense
Has left the world, as if she was a priest.
So two are saved from death, and, by that grace,
Four live for one another; grace sets out
Alone, and on the journey, one by one,
Gathers the lonely to a company
That sings at evening in the inn of heaven!

Moritsugu
So mercy spreads from soul to soul like flame,
And soon the world is an enormous beacon
Joining the host of heaven's scattered campfires!

Katsuyori
This was a sacred action, that will echo
As long as love is in the universe.

Moritsugu
How can we thank our Empress and our Lord
For bringing back my brother from the dead,
And sending Yokobue for your son?

Katsuyori
We can do nothing but succumb to love,
Like stars that effortlessly burn and shine.

Moritsugu
Our state will be a burst of light forever,
An endless blaze, an everlasting sunrise.

Lady Tonase
I am the beggar at this celebration,
I can admire and almost share your gladness,
But when my eyes return to what I am,
I am ashamed and suddenly alone.
There is a man more evil than a demon
Behind this business, and the joyful outcome
Cannot eclipse the evil he intended.
Oh God! I love my brother Morotaka
As mothers love their sons, and to be shown
His vicious nature in the same clear mirror,
Altered so suddenly, is hard to bear.
Lord Shigemori and Her Majesty,
Whose minds contain the world, will certainly
See what he is as well as you and I.
It is my terror that their view of me
Will darken in the shadow of my brother.
If I must share his downfall, so I will,
But all the gods and Buddha can attest
That I am innocent. But still I fear
That after I am dead, my reputation
Will be an everlasting slander. Sirs,
I only ask you for your sympathy.

Katsuyori
Lady Tonase, your experience
Is the more common one, and we descend.
Acknowledging your loss. But look, the grace
Lord Shigemori and Her Majesty
Have spread will certainly extend to you,
Lady Tonase. If they see the world
And all its secrets at a single glance,
Then they have seen not only the behaviour
Of Morotaka, but your innocence.
Our rulers have good eyesight, we are lucky,
And we should celebrate; the dreadful truth
Of the real world is honesty for us,
And freedom, and we live where love maintains
A crystal empire that the light adores.

Moritsugu
And yet these lovers have been saved from death
By separation, by religious vows,
And they survive in sorrow. We must pray
To heaven, that has half delivered them,
To find a way to set them free completely,
Farewell, my lady.

Lady Tonase   Thank you sir, farewell.

Katsuyori
Farewell, my lady.

Lady Tonase   Thank you sir, farewell.

Exeunt.

Scene Ten

Kwazan, outside the city, where **Yokobue** *has been sequestered.*
Night. Enter **Yokobue**.

Yokobue
   I have sorrowed at Kwazan
   For six years,
   Near the city, but alone,
   I watch the sun break into stars.

   Where is the moon tonight,
   Has she been hidden,
   Like myself, out of sight,
   Forgotten, forbidden?

   I see her expensive tears
   Littering the whole sky;
   If she herself appears,
   I will ask her why.

   Is she alone like me,
   Caught by a far-away light,
   Tied to a hysterical sea,
   Adorning infinite night?

Enter the **Moon**

Oh moon, forgive me; for the thousandth time
I have to ask you why I am alive.

Moon
You are alive because you are not dead.

Yokobue
But surely it is wrong to be alive
If I am banished from the one I love.

Moon
Banished? But why?

Yokobue   I told you yesterday.
Remember?

Moon   No, I have no memory.

Yokobue
He is a priest.

Moon   I hardly think that matters!

Yokobue
I would have said so once, I loved and loved,
Ignoring order, and because I did,
The entire nation almost lost its head.

Moon
Girl, come with me; are you a tree? Be moved!
Sway forwards, slip towards me like the sea,
Wander away from this delusive place!

Yokobue
Where are we going? Let me get my hat!

Moon
Hat? Does the sunrise hesitate for hats?
Does the sea stop and turn into a lake
Because the moon is looking for her hat?
Hurry!

Yokobue   But I must bid this place goodbye,
Where I have prayed in sorrow for six years,
Longing to leave.

Moon   Unbind its thatch that clings
To your rich hair –

Yokobue   These walls are like my brothers –

Moon
Remove the brickwork from your bones, come on,
Crack the foundations in your veins, tear down
The heaviness of dwelling from your mind!

Yokobue
Gone – I am gone – I have set out, departed,
Leaving the door wide open to the dawn,
To slam and splinter in whatever wind
Should happen to be passing. Oh strange light
Moment of flight! As when the autumn prodding
At swallows cancels out their gravity,
And they are lifted by the wind like songs.
Where are we going?

Moon   Somewhere over there –
I am so vague – I never can remember
The names of places, though I try. I am
The oldest baby in the universe,
Still staring in amazement at the light.

Yokobue
I have to find my lover Takiguchi.

Moon
Look at that mountain!

Yokobue   Izumi Shikibu
Wrote about that – it is so far away
In the warm south that it is still in autumn,
While we are feeling winter. Mount Inari,
The memory of love, the crimson mountain.

Moon
Oh, in a minute I will fade – the dawn

Steps suddenly into a million dreams,
A figure with a face too bright to see,
Ringing a bell to wake the hemisphere.
Villages bark themselves awake.

Yokobue   That village
Is Fukakusa; Shosho came from there,
Who died for love of Ono-No-Komachi,
The poetess. 'I shall not tell the wind
My name, time blows in the susuki grass.'

Moon
I am so faint, I am the memory
Of your great-great-great-grandmother, an O
Of blue-white lichen on a sky blue stone.

Exit.

Yokobue
I am in Gojo, where the flower sellers
Creak by in carts heaped high with irises.
Oh, it was riding in a cart that Genji
Came to the peasant girl. I have escaped;
Sunlight is now the owner of the house
My sorrows filled with shadows for six years;
The sun inspects his latest property,
Measures its emptiness with beams, leaps down
The stairs in one bound, uses all the windows
At once. He will invite his friend the wind
To press his mouth against the bending panes,
And they will call in spider decorators.
Why did I stay there for so long, a seed
Under a stone? What whisper made me leave?
A mystery – the making of this day
Required the labour of two thousand dawns,
Skilfully building up their glittering,
To make a lamp for me, which I must use.

Enter a **Peasant Girl**.

Excuse me, I have walked all night; please tell me,
Where have I got to?

Girl   This is Saga, lady.

Yokobue
Saga is famous for its hermitages,
Is that not right?

Girl   I should expect it is,
There are about a million of them here,
Each with a thousand priests.

Yokobue   But do you know
A certain one; he is a friend of mine,
A priest who was a samurai before.
Which is his temple, could you show me it?

Girl
Oh let me see. We get a lot of them.
You don't know what he changed his name to? No.
A priest who was a samurai before?
Who can it be? Oh! Father Nensai! No,
He was a baker, not a samurai.
And Father Dokin was a murderer
Before he was a priest. And Father Dosai
Has moved to Nara. Oh! A samurai?
Could he be from the Taira family?
A young man? Yes, some years ago a fellow
Shaved off his hair and joined the little temple
Of Ojoin, first right, straight down the lane.
Listen and you can hear him chanting now.

Yokobue
Thank you!

Girl   Oh well I don't suppose it's him.
The best of luck to you.

Yokobue   God bless you, thank you!

Exit **Peasant Girl**. *Enter* **Servant**.

Servant
Are you delivering the rice?

Yokobue   To whom?

Servant
The priest, my master.

Yokobue   I have come to see him,
But I have not brought rice.

Servant   Oh, just yourself!
Well, he won't touch it, so you can forget it,
He is a priest, he was a samurai,
He's young and so forth but he's disciplined,
Nothing at all for him, he wouldn't go
So far as to remove your packaging.
Ah, you delicious girls, who spend your time
Tempting the starving priests, you're terrible.
But I myself have taken no such vows
As make them thin, and I will taste your feast,
Out of politeness, if the cost is modest.
What have you got there? Peaches, warm buns, cherries –

Yokobue
I am your master's friend, I know him well,
He will resist temptations, having sworn,
With everlasting discipline, of course,
But if he sees me he will recognise me,
And he will not refuse to speak to me.

Servant
You know him, do you? Well you might have told me.
Embarrassed. Wait here.

Exit. Sound of banging and crashing, oos and ows from the **Servant**.
Re-enter **Servant** *very bashed about.*

                        Wonderful. Terrific.
What, are you still here? That was terrible.
I say, 'A girl has come to see you, sir,
She says she knows you.' He is at his prayers,
But he leaps up in rage and starts to shout,
And hits me with the hammer that he uses
To clang his bell with. He's incensed with me
Because I make the girls enjoy themselves
By being brash, but that's not my fault, is it?

I'm like a pot of honey in the sun,
They swarm around me and in vain I cry,
Leave me alone, you drive my master mad!

Yokobue
Your master is correct to be affronted
By the arrival of a female, forcing
Her way unchecked into his meditations.
And I am sorry for your pains, but tell him
That I am from the palace of the Empress.

Servant
No! You completely fail to understand!
It doesn't matter how well dressed you are,
He won't undress you, even if your skin
Is kissed by silk all over, and the silk
Covered with gold. No matter who you are,
You are a woman, and this priest is chaste.
Forget it darling.

Yokobue   You have shaved your head,
To serve your master in his change of life.
Heaven will bless you! But it must be cold.
Poor man! I wish I had a hood for you,
But I do not. But as a small reward
For your hard work, perhaps you will permit me
To give you this.

Gives him a cloth wrapper.

Servant   This is a costly item.
Crepe on the outside and a red silk lining.
Thank you, my lady, I can easily
Wrap it around my head. Was it a wrapper
For something else before, like gold and silver?

Yokobue
It was indeed, well guessed. It held much gold,
But on my way I emptied it to beggars.
But I will bring you anything you want,
When I return here. Tell me what you lack.

Servant
Oh, I lack nothing but a magic wand
To turn my dreams into reality.
Which gold can do.

Yokobue   Then I will bring you gold.

Servant
Then I will risk it, hoping not to be
His clapper's yelping bell again, announcing
To the surroundings his religious frenzy.

Exit.

Yokobue
Oh robin shouting in the elder tree,
The anger of your song needs no translation,
Is it the winter you are raving at,
Or is the object of your fury me,
For speaking with my love through bribery?

Re-enter **Servant**.

Servant (*imitating his master*)
Begone! No female creature with her foul
Beauty shall stir the mud of meditation
In which my master like a frog in winter
Sleeps undisturbed by fantasies of April.
No bitch, no mare, no fat Queen ant, no vixen
Shall breathe a ripple or by peering over
Stain his calm surface with her vain reflection.
Amphibious between the world and heaven,
He dreams, and he has no desire to spawn.
Remove forever from our sphere's perfection
The burden of the beauty of the world.

(*As himself.*)
Beautiful woman, thank you for the wrapper!
I am so sorry! Are you broken-hearted?
Cry for a while then find another lover!

Exit.

Yokobue

Another lover, like another coin
Stained by a thousand hands, to be exchanged
For a few mouthfuls of security!
No, I have finished with this life. My troubles
Have killed my spirit, and my emptiness
Distracts the blessed from their meditations.
Three years we yearned, and then we came together
In danger of destruction; but we swore
That death would never part us. Though rejected,
My soul is in the image of our vow,
And I cannot forget. So I will sink
Into this lake, and it shall be my eyes,
And it will be my bliss that his reflection,
Coming and going, is my spirit's colour.

Exit. Re-enter **Servant**.

Servant

Oh Heavens!
Master Come Quick. She's jumped in the pond.
Come on!
Rescue her, master, seize her in your arms!

Enter **Yoshitsugu** *in hood.*

Yoshitsugu
What are you saying?

Servant   Quickly! Over there!

Yoshitsugu
Oh! Buddha and the gods! Step back, step back!

Exit.

Servant

Ah! Saved her! Ah! She's fainted in his arms!
Oh lovely, lovely! Oh, you clever girl!

Re-enter **Yoshitsugu** *carrying* **Yokobue**. *She comes to.*

Yokobue
Oh Takiguchi, darling! Takiguchi!
Why did you send me from your presence, why?

Yoshitsugu
I am not Takiguchi.

Yokobue   Oh my darling,
No more pretending!

Yoshitsugu   I am Yoshitsugu,
And you are Yokobue. Yokobue!
Lord Shigemori stopped my execution;
Your saviour must have been Her Majesty.

Yokobue
But I have only called my life salvation
Because I dreamed of finding Takiguchi.
You are my friend, oh, kill me, Yoshitsugu!

Yoshitsugu
You could have been Karumo, Yokobue.

Yokobue
This is her grief. Wherever she may be,
These are her tears. I cry to Yoshitsugu
For Takiguchi. Somewhere in the world
Karumo weeps like me for Yoshitsugu,
Perhaps to no one. If she saw the face
To which I cry, her tears would turn to laughter;
And if the face in my imagination
Replaced the one I see, that sees my sorrow
And suffers equal grief, I would be happy.

Yoshitsugu
I cannot stay here having seen Karumo
Weeping to see me from another's eyes.
Buddha is everywhere. To leave this place
Is simply to attend a wider shrine.

Yokobue
So we shall cry, a curlew and a lapwing
Flying together, searching for our lovers.

They set out. Weather changes to a dreadful storm.

Yoshitsugu
Absence blows bitter from the peak of Hiei,

Carving the air along the mountain paths,
And its sharp fingers shock the mind and shuffle
The autumn pile of memories, that, whirling
In a mad waltz, confuse their images.

(*To* **Yokobue**.)
Oh my Karumo, when I sent my servant
To frighten you away, I was in terror;
It was because Lord Shigemori's wisdom
In saving us seemed so exactly balanced
But love has tipped it over, shattered it.

Yokobue
The crying of your ghost, my Takiguchi,
Is like the howling of the wind. My love,
We must forget the past. In this cold limbo
Where our souls blow, at least we are together.
When we are born into the world again,
Perhaps it will be better. I remember
It was impossible to love before,
Love was destruction and disunity.
Here on death's mountain we are cold but free.
My love, where are you?

Yoshitsugu   Keep in sight, keep up!
Do not fall back or we will lose each other!

Yokobue
What does it matter? We are like the wind,
We can divide across the universe
And still be lying in each other's arms.

Yoshitsugu
It is a tunnel, we must struggle through it.

Yokobue
It is a plateau, we can drift across it.

Yoshitsugu
Stand up! Stand up!

Yokobue   But I am far above you.

They look at each other in recognition.

Oh, Yoshitsugu, it is you, I think
You were my brother in another life.

Yoshitsugu
Oh Yokobue, it is only you,
Dear heart, keep walking, we are nearly there.

Yokobue
How terribly you sorrow for Karumo.

Yoshitsugu
How utterly you long for Takiguchi.

Yokobue
I have a present for my friend Karumo,
And she will love me when I give you to her.

Yoshitsugu
When I present my comrade Takiguchi
With you, I will have saved his life in battle.

Yokobue
We will survive if we can shelter here.

They approach a lighted door, at which a **Boy** *appears.*

Yoshitsugu
Young boy, young boy, may we take shelter here?
We are two travellers, no more than that
Lost in the snow; if we could beg a corner –

Boy
No. The priest said that when he is away
I am to let in no one. I am sorry.

Yoshitsugu
You are correct to guard the house so bravely,
It is the hungry season, when the door
Must frown on wolves and thieves. But look, and see,
The woman who is with me is unwell,
We will become the food of wolves ourselves,
The slaves of thieves, unless you pity us.
Young boy, forgive me if I burden you
With adult terms, but it would be a work
Of holiness for you to shelter us.

We will say sorry when the priest returns,
And you will not be blamed. Again I beg you,
Shelter us.

Boy   No, I cannot let you in.

Yoshitsugu
Then will you give us some of that hot water?

Boy
It is not water, it is medicine.
It is not ready.

Karumo (*within*) Are they travellers?
Oh, Kamawake darling, let them in,
The priest will soon be back.

Boy   I cannot do it.
That is my mother, she is ill in bed.
The priest is only in the nearby village,
I will run down and fetch him if you like,
But you must wait outside until he comes,
In case you try to carry off my mother.

Exit.

Yoshitsugu
Thank you! A fire in sight; oh, Yokobue,
Are you all right until the priest gets back?
Have every shred of clothing I can spare.

He lays his cloak down and **Yokobue** *lies on it.*

Speak to me! Should we overrule the boy,
Push through the door and lie you by the fire,
Where its invisible embrace extends
Motherly arms – but when the priest arrived
He would be angry, and for one short theft
We would have lost a freely given night.
We must obey the law the boy ordains,
Though even now observance of the letter
Risks losing heaven; freedom once again
Beckons us to the chasm. Oh my friend,
It is like love to see you shivering,

Breathing in pain. I press myself against you,
Frantic to keep the cold out. Oh this cold,
It is as strong as absence. Yokobue!

Enter **Boy** *and* **Takiguchi**.

Takiguchi
Who calls that name? Can it be Yoshitsugu!

Yoshitsugu
Can it be Takiguchi?

Takiguchi   Come inside!

They enter. **Takiguchi** *goes to fire with* **Yokobue**. *Enter*
Karumo.

Yoshitsugu
Karumo!

Karumo
Yoshitsugu!

They embrace, and **Karumo** *shows* **Yoshitsugu** *his son.*

But Yokobue – is it Yokobue?
My darling darling!

Takiguchi   She is hardly breathing.
But surely kisses will revive her, surely –
Oh my dear heart, where does your spirit wander,
Did your soul stumble out of your cold body
Somewhere along the mountain path? My darling,
Fire cannot warm you, it can only burn,
And though my spirit howls like a whole mountain
Splitting the wind, your body cannot hear!

Karumo
But wait, I have a precious medicine,
That was a present from Her Majesty
To Yokobue and myself, to say
That death on death will never part us three.
I think that if I burn it it will call
The spirit back into the dying body.

She unwraps the **Empress**'s *medicine, which is an incense stick. She burns it and immediately the* **Moon** *and the* **Titmouse** *appear, but not to* **Takiguchi**, **Yoshitsugu** *and* **Karumo**, *who remain bent over* **Yokobue**.

Moon
Where were you at dawn today?

Titmouse
That is very hard to say.
When I got there it was night,
But when I woke the place was bright.

Moon
Was it the old sun or another?

Titmouse
It was the old sun's younger brother.

Moon
The sun is getting very young.

Titmouse
That is exactly what I sung.

Moon
Was the world born yesterday?

Titmouse
No, this morning, so they say.

Moon
So has eternity begun?

Titmouse
According to the younger sun.

The **Moon** *sees a card on the ground and picks it up and reads it.*

Moon
Yokobue, Yokobue,
Open your eyelids like a daisy,
Wake up! Shake off tears of dew,
Love is bending over you.

Moon *and* **Titmouse** *exeunt.* **Yokobue** *wakes up.*

Yokobue
Oh, Takiguchi!

They embrace. **Karumo** *sees that something is written on the medicine wrapper. She reads.*

Karumo
Though a rock divides the river
Into streams that rush apart,
They will join again forever
In the sea's unbroken heart.

Yoshitsugu
Heaven has led us through a dream of death
To one another, and transformed our prayers
From broken cries to a united song,
Like the four corners of the world in one,
A prayer of power. We should leave this mountain,
And make our home among the harvest fields,
And as they grow we will petition heaven
To reconcile us with our Lord and Lady.

Exeunt.

Scene Eleven

Otsu, the temple of Sanno and Myojin. Enter **Morotaka**, **Genkuro** *and* **Muzo**.

Morotaka
Wider and wider freedom sets me free,
Beyond the end! The sea would eat the land
If it was free to do so. Yesterday
My freedom satisfied me utterly,
And yet compared to what I feel today,
It was a pitch black cell. And so I grow,
A wish and then an egg and then a bird,
And then the whole sky, over everything!
Lord Shigemori had to banish me,
He would have killed me, but respect and mercy
Bound him in double chains, and through my sister,

Lady Tonase, I was spared, my boys,
To be an outlaw here in Karasaki,
Robbing the pilgrims and the priests with you.
We take the silver that was meant for gods,
We know no fear, and if the tiny circle
Of a rope noose shall be our final empire,
In our wild lives we will have known more joy
Than those who bow to the invisible!
There will be many supplicants today.
I will stay here and, in the priest's attire,
Meekly receive the sacred offerings.

Morotaka *disguises himself as the priest. Enter* **Lady Tonase.**

Lady Tonase
Good priest, Her Majesty the Empress sends me,
Commanding what I would desire, to pray
For Takiguchi and for Yoshitsugu,
Two wrongly punished former samurai,
Now priests, and for two former maids of honour
Now banished, Yokobue and Karumo.
They have been seen here recently together,
Praying no doubt to Sanno and Myojin
To reconcile them with their Lord and Lady.
Lord Shigemori and Her Majesty,
Desiring this no less, have undertaken
To ask the gods through me to reunite them.

Morotaka
Oh gods of shadow and reflection, thank you
For sending me this way to stretch my freedom
Still wider, by a crime against my sister!

He forces her down onto the floor.

Lady Tonase
Help me!

Morotaka   Donate your money to the shrine
Of Morotaka, everything you have!

Lady Tonase
Oh! Help! Help! Robbery! Assault! Help! Help!

You are a demon, you are not my brother,
To buy my freedom back from hell's possession
There is no price I would not pay; however,
My money is not here.

Morotaka   No money on her,
Where is it then!

Lady Tonase   In Otsu at the inn.

Morotaka   We will return, my lady, very soon!

Exeunt **Morotaka**, **Muzo** *and* **Genkuro**, *leaving* **Lady
Tonase** *bound and gagged and covered with a cloth in the shrine.*
Enter **Takiguchi**, **Yokobue**, **Karumo**, **Yoshitsugu**,
Kamawake, *in solemn prayer.*

Yokobue
You gods of love and honour in the sun,
Who speak to us through changes in the sky,
Uncloud us; we have thought until our thoughts
Made a great wall that crowded out the light,
But we have ceased these efforts, and, confessing
The sin of praying to themselves, our minds
Collapse to holy silence, listening.
We only ask that through your excellence
You make a way for us to serve with honour
The love in us we cannot disobey.
So bless us that our love of one another
And of our Lord and Lady run together.

Karumo
Someone is crying!

Yoshitsugu   In the shrine!

Takiguchi
Lady Tonase!

They release her.

Karumo   Oh, abominable!
Who put you there, my Lady, who attacked you?

Lady Tonase
A devil in the shape of Morotaka,
My brother – no, a demon he created
From his own soul to make his crimes immortal!
But he is coming back!

Karumo   When he returns,
I will be lying in the shrine,
I will disarm him.

Takiguchi   We will ambush him.

Yoshitsugu
I will pretend to be the ferryman.

Yokobue
Hide, quickly, here he comes.

Exeunt, **Yoshitsugu** *into the boat,* **Karumo** *into the shrine,
covered with the cloth. Enter* **Morotaka** *out of breath.*

Morotaka
Absolute power – absolute impatience!
Sister! They would not listen at the inn,
Although I am your brother, whom you love,
And they refused to let me take your money.
You have to write a note immediately,
Ordering them to give me everything –
Heaven! Karumo! Am I in a dream?

Karumo
Sir, you deserve whatever you desire,
Because you know no fear. You are a hero;
Heaven is not for men who hesitate,
But for the fearless, who believe their dreams,
And drag them out into reality.

Morotaka
Where is my sister?

Karumo   She has run away;
I set her free. And when she told me, crying,
How you had threatened her with death and bound her,
And flung her, gagged, into the shrine,

My blood began to thunder in my ears,
My love for you, that I had fought to hide,
Rose up and broke the prison of my heart,
Rebelled in all my veins, and tore down caution.

Morotaka
How did you get here?

Karumo   When our dreams come true,
We either seize them and are crowned with life,
Or stand bewildered by the mystery,
And watch them sail away. My fate has brought me
Alone, and tortured by desire, to you;
I did not run when I had freed your sister,
Although I know that you are merciless;
Trembling, I climbed into the shrine,
To wait to be destroyed or to be taken.
So I accepted what my fortune gave,
Which was the first of many a surrender
(I hoped with all my heart) to your fierce power.
But I can see that you are not so sure.
Perhaps your love for me has died?

Morotaka   Karumo!
Am I alive or dead? It does not matter,
Whatever world this is, I worship it,
And it adores me! Welcome to my fortune,
Join me in my career, which is desire,
I grant you freedom, it is mine to give.
Let us consume each other utterly!

Karumo
Yes! But not here. We should he happier
If we could find an island in the lake,
With nothing but the kisses of the waves
Against its edges to disturb our passion!

Morotaka
Karumo, you are right. And where the sky
Lies on the water, we will lie together.
I see a boat! But surely I have died,
And this good fortune is my life's reward,

Payment for all my suffering. Here, boatman!
We are the spirits of true lovers, row us
To Ishiyama, would you? We will rise
As stars tonight, in one another's arms.

Yoshitsugu
Of course! I saw at once that you are lovers.
It is my privilege to ferry you,
And there will be no fee. Come, step on board!

Karumo
We are in heaven! Thank you, ferryman!

Yoshitsugu
One at a time, please. Beauty first, of course.

Karumo *steps into the boat, taking* **Morotaka**'s *staff with her.*
Yoshitsugu *pushes off.*

Yoshitsugu
And off we go!

Morotaka   Stop!

Yoshitsugu   Whoops! I'm sorry, sir,
But I prefer her on her own.

Morotaka   Karumo!
Scratch out his eyes and push him overboard!
Slave-trader! I will rescue her, no matter
How deep the water is. My darling! Demon!
I will wade out and kill him.

Yoshitsugu   Morotaka!
Look at me now, you know me!

Morotaka   Yoshitsugu!

Yoshitsugu
I have bad news. You will not get to heaven
Unless you kill yourself. Your life of shame
Deepens your condemnation every day.
In your next life you were to be a spider,
Before you tied your sister up so tightly,
Now you will be a tiny fly – tomorrow,

Perhaps a tic. You have to kill yourself.
Kill yourself!

Morotaka   It will not be me I kill,
When I suck up this lake and spit you out.
It is too deep! Oh I will turn to flame
And dry it to its bed. I will devour you,
Even if you escape into the sky,
My rage will overwhelm the lights of heaven
With the black smoke of the whole world on fire!

Takiguchi, **Lady Tonase**, **Kamawake** and **Yokobue**
appear.

Takiguchi
It would be better if you killed yourself.

Morotaka
My enemies surround me! Takiguchi!

They fight, **Morotaka** *is subdued and held down*.

I can still hate you!

Takiguchi   That hurts you, not me.

Morotaka
You shall not bind me!

Morotaka *is gagged and bound. Enter* **Yoshitsugu**, **Karumo**,
Kamawake, **Yokobue**.

Yoshitsugu
We cannot kill him, since Lord Shigemori
Saw fit to punish him by banishment.

Takiguchi
No need to kill him, let his hate devour him.

Lady Tonase
Here come the others, his accomplices!

Yoshitsugu
Hide and attack them.

They throw **Morotaka**, *covered with the cloth, into the shrine and
exeunt. Enter* **Muzo** *and* **Genkuro**.

Muzo   Where is Morotaka!

(*To the shrine.*)
Respected Lady, you have made us run
To Otsu, missing half a morning's takings,
And all the way back here again for nothing.
For this discourtesy you have to die.

*They stab the person under the cloth in the shrine and remove the cloth to
reveal* **Morotaka**. *They flee in horror.*

Ambush!

They flee. **Takiguchi** *and* **Yoshitsugu** *leap out, followed by the
others.*

Takiguchi
No need to chase them, terror of this day
Will drive them to the mountains, let them go.

Lady Tonase *kneels by the body of* **Morotaka**.

Yokobue
Lady Tonase –

Lady Tonase   This is not bereavement,
This is new hope. It comforts me to see
My bad blood creeping cowed into the ground,
Out of my brother's body. He is gone,
Now there is no descent from love. I know
That once he almost mesmerised the rivers
Of love in you to mud and you believed
That your desires were wrong, unseasonal
Disasters to the state. And so you prayed
At times for death, because the very sun
Seemed to have stopped suspended in mid-air.
Wrong – and his body only now by dying
Speaks through its wounds the truth his life belied,
Which you embody living. Love may cause
Disturbances and strife, but if it does,
That is because the briefest glimpse of it
Next to grey nothing, makes that nothingness
By contrast evil. If a person sees

Love in another that he lacks himself,
He hates and fights it. So with Morotaka,
But he is gone, and love is love again.
Lord Shigemori and Her Majesty
Desire you to return if you desire,
To be their strong and beautiful example.

They join hands.

Enter the **Moon**.

Moon

If you ask me why
Does my narrow eye
Grow so wide and round,
Silvering the ground,

What can I reply?
If your eyes could see
How it looks to me,
Staring through the sky

At the whole of life —
Like a well-dressed groom
Stepping from the tomb
To delight his wife —

You would stare like me,
You would move the sea,
You would shine all night,
Crying tears of light.

Printed in the USA
CPSIA information can be obtained
at www.ICGtesting.com
LVHW041101171024
794057LV00001B/194